"If you can dream, you can achieve it"

C.S........

My best wish

Dr. S.R. Valentine

William Scruton

A Biography and Comprehensive Index of

his

Pen and Pencil Pictures of old Bradford

by

Simon Ross Valentine

First published March 2023
Themelios International &

Copyright Simon Ross Valentine
ISBN: 9798379003623

PEN AND PENCIL PICTURES

OF

Old Bradford.

(W. R. YORKS.)

By WILLIAM SCRUTON,

Author of "The Birthplace of Charlotte Brontë," etc.

[See page 243.]

WITH PLAN, PORTRAITS, AND OTHER ILLUSTRATIONS.

Bradford:

Title page of the original published edition, 1889

CONTENTS

Picture of William Scruton 7

Author's Preface 8

Introduction: Who was William Scruton? 10

Scruton: Historian, writer and artist 13

The reasons why Scruton wrote *The Pen and Pencil
Pictures of Old Bradford* 15

Pen and Pencil Pictures: A summary 17

The Sources used by Scruton in writing his book 25

The Index: house-style and explanatory notes 28

List of illustrations in Pen and Pencil Pictures 30

Index to Scruton's book 33

References 81

William Scruton 1840-1924
(Image, courtesy of Bradford Local Studies Library)

Preface

Pen and Pencil Pictures of Old Bradford, written by William Scruton and published in 1889, is a *tour de force*, providing a fascinating description of the social, political, religious and cultural life of a northern industrial town in Victorian England. Wide in its scope, and based on unique source material, Scruton's Work is an invaluable tool for both local and national historians. The publisher, Thomas Brear of Bradford, stated with alacrity that this is "one of our finest books on local history …. illustrated by sketches of many ancient buildings which disappeared in the reconstruction of the town about 1870-80".[1]

During my several decades of research into the history of Bradford, Scruton's beautiful book – and it is beautiful, with its numerous sketches, illustrations and photographs – has been for me a constant companion, a faithful guide and a reliable source of relevant information.

However, despite its obvious merits and appeal, the book can be frustrating for the researcher, chiefly because Scruton did not provide an index. Although detailed contents of chapters are given at the start of the book, the reader may well have to skim his or her way through the pages in an attempt to find material on featured persons, subjects and places. There are significant references to subjects such as Chartism, or places such as Bolling Hall throughout the book, but without the aid of an index, such references are difficult to find.

Although in the last few years several indexes have been completed for *Pen and Pencil Pictures,* regrettably, listing personal names only, they are greatly limited in their use. As such, there has been a real need for a comprehensive Index listing places, subjects, themes as well as personal names. This current volume – providing such a comprehensive Index plus a brief but informative biography of Scruton, an appraisal and summary of the book, and a list of illustrations used by Scruton - is an attempt to fill that gap.

In completing this Index gratitude is owed to certain institutions and people. Christine May, Head of Bradford Libraries & Archives and Caroline Brown, Local Studies & Archives Manager are to be thanked for their continuing support, and for permission to access and use library sources. It has been a pleasure working with the staff at the Local Studies Library, Bradford, where various staff members – in particular Simon Arnold, Robin Downes, and Jan Sykes - have been tireless in their efforts to "dig-up" material for me. Thanks go also to Fiona Marshall, Sarah Powell and Richard Brass, the staff at the West Yorkshire Archives for similar assistance. Finally, I thank my family and close friends for their constant support and encouragement.

Dr Simon Ross Valentine
Bradford
March 2023

Introduction: Who was William Scruton?

There were several historians of note in Victorian Bradford, local men with local interests who, in differing ways, provided invaluable insights into the economic, cultural and religious development of the town.

John James led the way with his *History and Topography of Bradford* (1841) and his *Continuation and Additions* to that History published twenty-five years later. In 1868, William Cudworth, at that time a journalist with the *Bradford Observer,* published his *Historical Notes on the Bradford Corporation.* He then began a regular series of articles in the *Observer* describing his informative "Rambles" around Horton, Bowling, Heaton, and other parts of the borough. These articles later formed the basis of his detailed book titled *Round About Bradford* published in 1876. Joseph Horsfall Turner, the schoolmaster of Idle, wrote about the different strands of Nonconformity in Bradford-dale. J. Norton Dickons, solicitor and antiquarian, and Thomas Thornton Empsall, the first President of the Bradford Historical & Antiquarian Society (BHAS), wrote papers on numerous aspects of life in nineteenth-century Bradford. These, and other writers, such as Abraham Holroyd, James Burnley, and James Parker did much to describe and preserve the history of Bradford as the town rapidly developed from a large village in 1800 to "Worstedopolis" the textile capital of the world, less than a century later.

William Scruton (1840-1924) - author, historian, antiquarian, and artist – was without a doubt one of the most important names in this list of notable Bradford historians. Up to the present day his main book, *Pen and Pencil Pictures of old Bradford,* remains one of the most popular, and widely read books on "bygone Bradford".

However, despite Scruton's importance as a historian, unfortunately, our knowledge of his life is limited. From Census reports we know he was born on 2 April 1840 in Little Horton Green, Bradford, and that he was the fifth child of Richard Scruton, a cordwainer (shoemaker) and Ada Scruton his wife.[2] We also learn that William had three brothers, James, John, and George and one sister, Ann.

One of the earliest influences on Scruton as a writer was probably his father. It is said that Richard Scruton, having lived "through stirring times" (including the Napoleonic Wars), was "fond of recounting events which lingered in his memory". William, from the earliest age ", was a ready listener" to these stories.[3] Later, when he was recognised as a reputable local historian, Scruton ascribed "his fondness for historic and antiquarian knowledge partly to the circumstance that his father not only possessed a fresh and vigorous intellect, but also a memory full of traditional lore".[4]

Other glimpses into Scruton's childhood are at hand. There is reason to believe that he had contact with the famous Bradford solicitor Samuel Hailstone, who lived at nearby Horton Hall. Hailstone, a learned and accomplished man, possessed one of the finest libraries in England. It seems Scruton, when just a young boy while performing errands and odd jobs, was an occasional visitor to the Hall, although terrified by the dogs Hailstone kept to guard his property.[5] It is also known that Scruton, from childhood, was always keen to hear the stories told by local people about the legends and tales of former days in Bradford.[6]

Scruton's life illustrates what John Ruskin, the famous art critic and social reformer called "the great art of getting on". Rather than a "rags-to-riches" story as seen in the lives of several successful Bradford entrepreneurs Scruton, raised in relative poverty, achieved considerable literary success by application, discipline and a thirst for reading and knowledge.

His formal education was meagre. Until his early teens, he attended a "Dame school" of which we have no details. Such institutions were run by a woman (usually elderly) in her own home where young children, for a small fee, received a rudimentary education, mainly reading, writing and arithmetic. Scruton, to improve his education, read any book he could lay his hands on. Such private reading and study were supplemented by attendance at public lectures. Throughout his working life, Scruton spent much time as an evening student attending the classes held at the Mechanic's Institute, then located at the corner of Well Street and Leeds Road.

Scruton, aged about twelve, began work as "a warehouse boy" for the firm of Milligan, Forbes & Co., whose warehouse on Hall Ings was until recently occupied by the Telegraph & Argus newspaper. As his education improved, so did his employment prospects. Scruton the "stuff warehouseman" later became the chief warehouse clerk. However, by the 1860s he had left the textile trade and obtained a well-paid position of legal clerk at the firm of Messrs Herbert J. Jeffery & Sons, solicitors, Cheapside, where he stayed for 59 years.

The Paper Hall, Barkerend
(Photograph S. R. Valentine)

An interesting anecdote has been passed down to us relating to Scruton's experience as a "warehouse boy". It is said that while working at Robert Milligan's warehouse on Hall Ings he occasionally spoke with W. E. Forster, the famous Bradford politician, the man largely responsible for introducing the Education Bill of 1870, which laid the foundation of our modern state education system. Forster's warehouse was next door to the one in which the young Scruton worked. As such Scruton often saw the celebrated MP arriving at and departing from his warehouse. "He always had a pleasant greeting for me", Scruton used to say. "Once he asked me what I was going to be when I became a man". Scruton replied that he intended to be either a soldier or a parson. "Why a soldier?", Forster asked. "Oh for the glory of it", Scruton replied. "And why a parson?". "Oh, because it is a nice easy-going respectable job", was Scruton's answer. Forster laughed at Scruton's youthful impertinence and then quietly remarked: "Take my advice, my lad, and don't be either. Get a good trade in your hands and push your way manfully in the world".[7]

As discussed below, although Scruton did not achieve business and commercial success as Forster probably meant, he did "push his way manfully in the world" as a writer and artist becoming an acknowledged historian of merit.

Concerning his personal life and character Scruton was a staunch member of the Moravian Church attending their Chapel in Little Horton Lane. A deeply religious man, he gave addresses at various local dissenting Churches and served for a time as a Sunday School teacher. As seen in his *Pen and Pencil Pictures* and other writings Scruton was tolerant of other denominations, particularly so of Roman Catholicism of which he wrote objective, if not sympathetic accounts.

Although tolerant of other faiths it was said that Scruton could at times be very officious and impatient with those "who feigned historical knowledge". In particular, as Jack Reynolds observed, Scruton "was recognised as friendly and helpful to others but known as a sharp critic of plagiarists who made use of his work without giving him proper acknowledgement".[8] Such a comment however seems a little harsh as it could be argued wouldn't anyone feel the same as Scruton if *their* work was plagiarised, especially for financial profit?

From the relevant Census Returns, we learn that in 1867 Scruton (aged 26/27) had married Ellen, a woman five years his junior, and they were living at 60 Rupert Street, Horton. By 1871 he and his wife had moved to Greaves Street, again in Horton, and had one child, a daughter Ada. Ten years later, in 1881 they were living at 35 Clough Street, Bowling, and had one more daughter, Maggie. Later, it appears William and his wife had another daughter, Marguerite. By 1911, with the improvement of Scruton's salary and status as a legal clerk, the Scruton family had moved to "Whitelands", 17 Station Rd, in the more respectable area of Baildon. The 1911 census indicates that by that year regrettably two of Scruton's daughters had died. Scruton himself died at St Luke's Hospital, Bradford, on 31 January 1924, aged 83 and was laid to rest in Scholemoor Cemetery.[9]

Scruton: historian, writer and artist

Scruton is rightly recognised today as a capable historian, writer and artist. One of his first attempts at authorship was an article on "The Old Inns and Hostelries of Bradford" printed in the *Bradford Observer*. This article later formed a chapter in his *Pen and Pencil Pictures of Old Bradford*. By the late 1870s, Scruton was a regular contributor, not only to the *Bradford Observer* but to other local newspapers such as *The Bradford Daily Telegraph, Yorkshire Notes and Queries* and *The Yorkshireman*. With years of research behind him on all aspects of local history, he contributed many articles to the *Bradford Antiquary*, the official journal of the BHAS, and also gave lectures at the society's meetings.

Scruton's first published book, titled The *Birthplace of Charlotte Brontë* (1884) proved to be a popular work running to three editions. Again, manifesting his deep interest in the Brontë family and their literary achievements Scruton brought out his *Thornton and the Brontës* in 1898. As a reviewer wrote in *Yorkshire Notes and Queries* "this book is beautifully illustrated, and is a fine specimen of typography".[10] In the year previous to the publication of *Thornton and the Brontës* Scruton, apparently at the suggestion of William Byles proprietor of the *Bradford Observer*, published his *Bradford fifty years ago* a jubilee memorial celebrating the gaining of borough status by the town. But his most well-known publication, and his most important contribution to the history of the locality, was unquestionably his *Pen and Pencil Pictures of Old Bradford* which is analysed and summarised below. Illustrated with upwards of a hundred sketches and portraits the first edition of *Pen and Pencil Pictures*, a run of a thousand copies, sold out rapidly.

Scruton was influenced and encouraged in his writing by William Cudworth. We know that Cudworth, an experienced journalist and historical writer, helped Scruton with his first article on Bradford Inns (mentioned above), and on later works. In the preface to his *Pen and Pencil Pictures* Scruton Informs us how: "Mr William Cudworth has been to me a 'Friend in council'". He states with obvious affection and gratitude:

"I cannot forget the words of encouragement received from him when making my first literary venture".

On that occasion Cudworth had said:

"I hail with pleasure your proposal to give something to the antiquarian world, as I feel sure you will not stop after your first essay'".[11]

Scruton was acquainted with, and probably influenced and encouraged by, other literary figures living and working in Bradford at that time. During the 1850s and '60s, we know he was a member of the group of *literati* that regularly met at the book-shop of the writer Abraham Holroyd in Westgate where new and old ideas were shared and discussed. Similarly, he attended the society of writers which met regularly at Tom Nicholson's dining room in Kirkgate. At such gatherings, Scruton spoke with a variety of successful literary figures including the aforementioned John James and William Cudworth but also with others such as the linguist and bibliophile Charles Antoine Federer and the poets Stephen Fawcett, James Waddington and Ben Preston.

In May 1878 Scruton, with Empsall and Cudworth, was one of the founding members of the BHAS. Throughout the remainder of his long life, he was actively involved in all aspects of the society serving initially as curator and the society's first librarian. During the society's first year, Scruton contributed a paper on "The Pictorial Illustration of Bradford", one of many articles he wrote on historical matters which were published in the *Antiquary*. Such articles were well-researched and authoritative. As Reynolds states, Scruton's:

"analysis of the Johnson Map of 1801 and the Atkinson plan of 1825, reported in the Transactions of the Society, still makes fascinating reading".[12]

Similarly Scruton's lecture on the Great Strike of 1825 "recalling the turbulent origins of Bradford's textile world" is still cited as an authority in modern-day journals and books.

As well as being a capable historian and writer Scruton was also an artist of considerable ability using this talent to record buildings and views in Bradford soon to disappear. He was a good sketcher and watercolour artist and many of his books, particularly his *Pen and Pencil Pictures*, are illustrated by his own hands. It is to Scruton that we are indebted for providing us with images of various former buildings in Bradford now long since demolished such as the Old Corn Mill, the Old Cock Pit, Bradford Old Bank, the Old Piece Hall, the White Swan Inn and the Quaker Chapel at Goodmansend.

Reasons why Scruton wrote The Pen and Pencil Pictures of Old Bradford

Scruton readily acknowledges John James' *History of Bradford* and James' *Continuation and Additions* as forming the standard history of the town. However, as Scruton explains, since the publication of James' books:

"So great a transformation has taken place, and the old has so completely given place to the new, that anyone revisiting Bradford after an absence of a quarter of a century would fail to recognise it, and would require the magic aid of Aladdin's lamp, or Fortunatus' cap, in wandering through its labyrinth of newly-formed streets and thorough-fares".[13]

Consequently, Scruton is greatly concerned:

This portrait was painted by John Sowden in 1909 when Mr. Scruton was about 69.

"Today how few of the relics of 'Old Bradford' remain to revive the 'lingering memories' of its old inhabitants, or to awaken the curiosity of its 'young and rising generation!'".[14]

Scruton is particularly scathing of the contemporary town planner and developer, the "house-building Philistine" as he calls them, "who, we fear, would have made short work of all that was ancient or sacred about it in his haste to 'run up' some ghastly pile of back-to-back houses".[15]

He laments how Bradford once a beautiful rural village, had become dominated by "chimney stacks belching out perpetual clouds of dingy smoke, and blast furnaces with fire leaping from their summit and glowing at their base, keeping up one ceaseless deafening roar by day and night".[16]

With these "great and rapid alterations that were being made in many parts of the town", Scruton was determined to preserve details (and images) of an "Old Bradford" rapidly disappearing. The danger of Bradfordians losing important aspects of their history and traditions was real yet, as Scruton stated in the "prospectus", the pre-publication leaflet for the *Pen and Pencil Pictures*:

"Little has been done as yet, in placing on record in a permanent form, the topographical, social, industrial, and biographical history of Bradford, and it will be the object of the present work to supply this long-felt want".

"Some years ago", continues Scruton, "it occurred to me that unless something was done and done without delay, to secure views of the principal places of interest, every trace of the same would be removed and the opportunity of preventing their utter annihilation gone forever". As such, he informs us how "with such ability as I possessed, I succeeded in taking views of many relics of historic interest, all traces of the existence of which might otherwise have been lost".[17]

"As to my qualifications", remarks Scruton modestly, "for such a task I need perhaps only state that my tastes have always had a strong tendency towards historical research, and that I have for several years back contributed articles to the local press, bearing upon the history of Bradford-my native town".[18]

But Scruton's ability to write such a book was never in doubt. Referring to one of Scruton's articles appearing in the *Bradford Antiquary*, a columnist in the *Bradford Observer* remarked:

"Mr., Scruton has a proper reverence for old places, old families, and old associations, and in his remarks contrives to arouse a deep interest in the mind of the reader. He is a most entertaining cicerone through the regions of the local past".[19]

Scruton was keen to produce "a popular volume at a popular price", omitting "nothing of interest pertaining to [Bradford's] history unless it be the minutiae of local archaeology or moot points of merely antiquarian interest". As such Scruton's aim in writing his *Pen and Pencil Pictures* was, as he said:

"To picture the town, both by pen and pencil, in all the periods of its history, and to journey hither through all the old streets and lanes, and into the old places of resort, now into the old religious sanctuaries in which our forefathers worshipped, and anon into the old theatres and other places where they found amusement and recreation, here in some old inn or hostelry among politicians and news-mongers, and there in the old workshops among toilers and artisans, from whose midst have sprung the men - worthy sons of worthy sires - who have made the Bradford that we behold today. The general appearance of the town prior to its recent transformation, its social and public condition, the home and industrial life of its inhabitants, its old families and worthies, its old customs, feasts and fairs, and its eccentric and odd characters will all come in for notice, and will be dealt with in a faithful, attractive and popular style".[20]

Scruton does not fail us in achieving this purpose.

Pen and Pencil Pictures: a summary

Scruton is a man who loved his home town (Bradford became a city in 1897). In his *Pen and Pencil Pictures of Old Bradford* he takes us on his "peregrinations" around the borough and, with his aid, we see the old "nooks-and-corners" of Bradford, and we meet some of the local people of by-gone days, the rich and the poor, the rational and those justifiably characterised as eccentric.

Beginning with a "brief historical survey" Scruton, in chapter one of the book, describes the first settlers in Bradford Dale from earliest times, through the Roman, Saxon and Danish invasions, to the Norman Conquest. Particular attention is given to the Domesday Book and the devastation caused by the Normans in the "harrying of the North". Relying mainly on the earlier works carried out by John James and Dr Whitaker, Scruton discusses the etymology of the name "Bradford", and how the town – no more than a hamlet in those days – gained royal charters to hold a market, fair, and Manor Court.

Scruton has a particular interest in the origins of Bradford parish Church dating it as early as 1281, and in the history of the leading families – the Tempests, Bollings, and Rawsons - during the Medieval period. He includes accounts of the constant threat of Scottish raids and that of the "greater enemy", the Black Death. Of necessity, Scruton recounts the legend of the Wild Boar of Cliffe Wood, the story of which to this day is represented in Bradford's official Coat of Arms.

Much of the first chapter is given to the events of the Civil War: the two sieges of Bradford, the occupation of the town by the Royalist commander the Earl of Newcastle, and the ghost of Bolling Hall – the "white lady" - pleading for the town with her memorable words "Pity poor Bradford". Scruton discusses how, although slow to recover from the Civil War, Bradford eventually turned from woollen manufacture to the production of worsted goods and how "soon after the middle of the eighteenth century, unmistakable signs of commercial prosperity appear". Reference is made to the building of banks (mainly due to the Quakers), the opening of the Piece Hall in 1774, followed "soon after by the formation of the Bradford canal".[21]

Scruton devotes the entire second chapter to a discussion of the Parish Church, and how the "Kirk in the woods" in Saxon times, underwent various extensions from the fifteenth century onwards, later becoming "the venerable St Peters". Interesting vignettes are given of the incumbents serving as Bradford's vicars such as the Puritan Caleb Kempe and the Royalist (some would say Roman Catholic) Francis Corker. Scruton provides us with "a succession of vicars who, if not distinguished for eccentricity of character, or excess of zeal, were, at any rate, men of learning and piety - holy men who went about their master's business".[22] Particular attention is given to John Crosse, the evangelical vicar, and friend of John Wesley; the "eminent career as scientist, Arctic explorer and philo-

Bradford Canal & the Parish Church

sopher" of the irascible and controversial Dr William Scoresby and the ecumenically minded Rev Henry Heap

Having discussed the ancient Parish Church, in the third chapter, under the title "Modern Churches", Scruton considers the other Anglican places of worship in Bradford. His focus of attention is on Christ Church, in Darley Street, St John's and St James' on Manchester Road, St John's in Bolling, and various other Anglican establishments. Individuals are focussed on also particularly Parson Bull of Bierley, the "Political Parson" so-called because of his energetic efforts in factory reform and the Ten Hour Movement. The 1851 census clearly showed that Nonconformity in Bradford was as strong if not stronger than the Established Church. Scruton describes the Ten Church Movement involving, as the name implies, the building of ten new Churches in the Bradford area by the Anglicans in their effort to "catch up" numerically with the other denominations.

Unlike some Nonconformists in Bradford who strongly opposed the "old religion" (there was a significant Orange Order in the town) Scruton ends the third chapter with a judicious account of the emergence and growth of Roman Catholicism in the region. Despite considerable opposition, Catholic immigrants from Ireland arriving in Bradford seeking employment and an escape from famine were (as early as 1825) celebrating Mass in their own Chapel, St Mary's, in Stott Hill. The public debates that took place between the Catholic clergy and dissenting and Anglican ministers – usually vitriolic and violent – are described and how, encouraged by the passing of the Catholic Emancipation Act 1829, Roman Catholics soon built other Churches in Bradford.

Scruton, himself an active Nonconformist (a Moravian preacher) uses chapter four to consider "the Dissenters" (Nonconformity and Dissent being interchangeable ecclesiastical terms). He describes the beginning of Nonconformity under the Act of Uniformity 1662 which caused 2,000 ministers to leave the Established Church due to their refusal to give their "unfeigned assent and consent" to the Book of Common Prayer. Scruton considers the life of one such ejected minister Jonas Waterhouse, the local vicar, and the hardships that he faced. Scruton argues that the meeting of dissenters organised by Thomas Sharp at Chapel Fold, Wibsey, was the "birthplace of Nonconformity in Bradford".[23] But of course, we can argue with him on this point referring to the dissenter's meeting at Kipping and other such meetings which predate Chapel Fold.

As in other parts of the book here in chapter four we are presented with interesting vignettes of different Dissenters. The portrayal of the eccentric Joseph Dawson - respected scientist and minister at Idle, one of the founders of the Low Moor Ironworks - gives us an idea of the vagaries of religious dissent.

In fairly quick succession, Scruton introduces the reader to the other dissenting denominations to be found in Bradford. The Quakers, facing severe persecution in the early years, later, due to their thrift, honesty and reliability, "became closely interwoven with the trading pursuits of the town" particularly wool-combing, banking and insurance. Concerning the Presbyterians and Congregationalists Scruton highlights *inter alia* the Horton Lane Chapel which, with many of Bradford's leading public figures attending, became, a veritable hot-bed of dissenting political power. Mention is made of the Baptists and how, from their humble beginnings as a house group in Manningham, established a wide network of Chapels, a theological college and boasted leaders of national prominence such as William Steadman and J. P. Chown. Wesleyan Methodism is presented, from the pioneering days of John Wesley, and John Nelson (and his incarceration in Ivegate dungeon), to the age of Methodist success and expansion, manifested in the erection of the impressive Kirkgate and Eastbrook Chapels.

But Scruton also considers the smaller, lesser-known Church groups such as the Swedenborgians (the so-called New Church) the followers of Emmanuel Swedenborg; the German Evangelical Church and of course his own denomination, Moravianism. Having discussed the various Dissenting groups in some detail it is then surprising that the Jewish community, although a highly significant group in the development of Bradford, is given only one brief paragraph. Similarly, the Catholic Apostolic Church and the Bible Christians merit only one sentence each.

Turning our attention away from religion Scruton, in chapter five, considers the educational and literary Institutions of Bradford. Pride of place is given to Bradford Grammar School (the boy's school mainly with a brief reference to the girl's school) before accounts are given of the Mechanics Institute, the Church Literary Institute, Philosophical Society, Bradford Subscription Library, Airedale College, and Horton Baptist College. Interesting insights are given to the work of Sunday schools, especially to John Brown, "a Wesleyan residing in Mill Bank, who in 1773 began a school in his own house and had about twenty scholars".[24]

Chapter VI is delightful, presenting in pictures and words, "the old public buildings" of Bradford. With an acute sense of loss and nostalgia Scruton describes some of the old buildings, "now gone forever", such as the old Court House "top of Westgate"; "Mr Lister's Court at Spotted House" in Manningham Lane, the old "lock-up" in Sunbridge, the earliest workhouse, and the old Piece Hall. An account is given of the "Cock-pit", dubbed as "the synagogue of Satan" due to the cock-fighting, gambling and other nefarious activities that took place within its walls, yet later used by various local religious groups for worship including the early Methodists. Useful insights are given regarding the origins of the Bradford Dispensary, the Infirmary and the Post Office that used to stand beneath the Parish Church in Forster Square.

Scruton's vivid account of the theatres in Bradford clearly reveals that, although a Nonconformist and a Moravian preacher, he did not exhibit the "Puritanical prejudices" against "the Play-House", and probably attended and enjoyed some of the theatres and plays he describes. With unrestrained alacrity he reminds his readers of "the periodical visits of such strolling companies as Holloways, Thornes, Parrish's, Chatterton's and others who for many years pitched their tents in such open places in the town as might be available".[25] Providing his own sketches, accounts are given of the animated performances of actors such as Mr Nunn, Mr J. D. Stoyle, Charles Rice and the "talented and precocious" Miss Maria B. Jones, "one of the brightest ornaments of the local stage".[26] He recalls the "strange and adventurous careers" of local and national thespians - Lysander Thompson and G. V. Brooke "whose tragic fate on board the *London* will long be remembered" and many others who trod the boards of the Theatre Royal in Duke Street and other local venues.[27]

As well as the old Bradford theatres Scruton devotes an entire chapter of the book (chapter VII) to "the old Inns and the coaching days" before the introduction of the railways. Again with beautiful sketches of several of the old hostelries, Scruton reminds his readership of how certain taverns, such as the Bull's Head Inn, were formerly used by merchants to "talk on politics and trade, forming themselves into a veritable Chamber of Commerce" or the Hope and Anchor Inn which was "linked with such useful organisations as Friendly Societies, Clubs (such as Bradford Cricket Club) and social gatherings for the development of various good objects". In other hostelries, supporters of political parties – the Tories, Whigs or Liberals – met during canvassing and elections. In the coaching days, such Inns were the "House of Call" where the "Highflyer", the "Duke of Leeds", the "Defiance" and "sundry other coaches passed through the town". However, as Scruton remarks, the "old coach-and-six" was rapidly superseded by the speed and convenience of the "steam locomotive", and inevitably "old established way-side Inns and posting houses became tenantless and deserted".[28]

Bradford, since the days of the Civil War, if not earlier, has always been a political as well as a religious hot-bed. Like most Nonconformists of that time Scruton had a keen interest in politics. References to the Reform Bill of 1832, factory reform, dis-establishment or the anti-slavery campaign are littered throughout the book. Manifesting laudable objectivity, and never flying a partisan flag, Scruton, in chapter VIII describes the campaigns, controversies and canvassing of "the early parliamentary elections" in Bradford. Objectively Scruton describes for us the election of 1832 and the appointment of the town's first two members of parliament: John Hardy and Ellis Cunliffe Lister. Other elections down to 1867 are discussed and the emergence of W. C. Lister, W. E. Forster and Sir Titus Salt as Bradford's MPs. Reference is made to Peter Bussey and the relative strength of Chartism in Bradford at that time. The chapter ends with a useful list of the candidates (unsuccessful as well as those elected) in these early election contests.

The succeeding chapters, replete with charm and quirkiness, reveal other aspects of life in Bradford. In chapter IX, for example, Scruton considers "old Bradford families and their homes". He gives us the histories of the old Mansions and Halls – Stott Hall, Manor Hall, Bierley Hall, Horton Hall - now demolished and gone forever and that of other Halls - the Paper Hall, Royds Hall, Bolling Hall - still standing today, but (except for Bolling Hall) only a shadow of their former glory. The families that occupied these mansions – the Rawsons, Sharps, Tempests, Hardys, Peckovers, Seebolms, and other manorial and manufacturing dynasties - are described and given credit for the contribution they made to the development of Bradford as a fascinating northern town.

This is followed by chapter X containing Scruton's reminiscences of "some old nooks and corners" of the town in particular the old shops and the shopkeepers found in them. Many of Scruton's readers would have had fond memories of Mr Tordoff, the tea-dealer; "dumb John" the barber (so-called because he rarely spoke); the spice seller Judy Barrett "and her world-famed humbugs" and a host of other retailers described with affection and respect.

Eager to present Bradford, not only as an industrial and manufacturing centre, but also as a place of culture and scholarship Scruton, in chapter XI considers "early literature and art" in the town. Artists, engravers, printers, journalists, poets, and sculptors – not encouraged at the time, and little known today - are paraded before the reader and praised for their work. Printers such as the Wardmans and the Nicholsons (who were also poets of repute such as John Nicholson, the "Airedale poet"); the journalist and newspaper editor William Byles; the Brontë sisters, and local artists J. C. Bentley, John and Charles Cousen and William Overend Geller, a painter and engraver of national repute. There is mention also of Patrick Branwell Bronte who, despite his troubled life was a painter of some ability,

The old shops at the bottom of Kirkgate

The book ends with a short chapter depicting "some notable and odd characters" found in the Bradford area. After a brief discussion of astrologers and fortune tellers, "who were plentiful enough and who made it a 'paying business'" Scruton turns our attention to the enigmatic "prophet John Wroe" of Bolling. With his long beard, unkempt clothes and hair, and riding on a donkey Wroe made predictions (some of which came true) and organised the local Southcottians, later forming the cult of British Israelitism.

Accounts of other unusual Bradford characters then follow: Jonas Tasker known locally as the "eccentric verger" due to his penchant for debate and grumbling over a pint in local pubs; and "Blind Jimmy" (James Mortimer) of Heaton who despite his disability didn't just beg for a living but at set times and locations entertained the passers-by by skilfully playing hymn-tunes on his clarinet. Last but not least mention is made of the "old Christmas Waits", particularly to Samuel Smith, otherwise known as "Blind Sam" who, with three colleagues (also blind) and another sighted person as a guide, walked around Bradford at Christmas playing tunes on their musical instruments. With these images and cameo portraits of local odd characters, Scruton concludes his book leaving the reader with a warm appreciation, and a nostalgic longing for a "bygone Bradford", much of which has vanished forever.

The sources used by Scruton in writing his book

It has been said with justification that a historian is only as good as his sources. The sources used by Scruton – letters, public documents, diaries, and ecclesiastical records - were accurate, reliable and varied. Scruton, as mentioned above, lacked a university education, receiving a knowledge of history, literature and politics in the evening classes he attended at the Mechanic's Institute and in disciplined private study. Despite this he was unquestionably a thorough and able historian, writing articles and books of academic and artistic merit. As a good historian, he used invaluable primary sources as well as relevant books written later about Yorkshire.

In writing about the Medieval period Scruton referred to various contemporaneous historical documents such as the account compiled by Simeon, the Chronicler of Durham describing William the Conqueror's "harrying of the North"[29]; the Poll Tax of Richard II to gain details of Bradford residents at that time, and to "certain Bradford Wills ranging from 1420 to 1560" to show the nature of the Parish Church and its clergy.[30] Possibly Scruton knew some Latin as he makes considerable use of Court Rolls of the fourteenth century and the "extant wills kept at York", and other ecclesiastical records.[31] The thoroughness of his research is seen in his occasional reference to "a document of ancient date" to consider "vicarial dues" or to "the discovery of an ancient record in the York Archiepiscopal registers".[32] As indicated above the two most important secondary sources used by Scruton were the

Histories written by Dr Whitaker, and that of "the sage historian" John James.[33]

Scruton was equally as thorough in his research on later periods as he was with the Medieval. For the sixteenth and seventeenth centuries appropriate reference is made to John Leland, "the topographer" and the travel details in his *Itinerary* (1536-42), and to William Dugdale's "*Visitation*" of Yorkshire (1665).[34] The description of the Civil War, and the two sieges of the town during that conflict, is largely based on Fairfax's *Memoirs*, Markham's *Life of the Great Lord Fairfax,* and the account provided by a Bradford resident during that tumultuous time, Joseph Lister.[35]

Prophet John Wroe of Bolling

Like any capable local historian today Scruton made good use of the Census Reports from when they began in 1801. Also, forming cordial links with various local people and institutions he gained access to "documents now in possession of Mr., Edward Hailstone"; the autobiography of Thomas Wright, of Birkenshaw and the "Warden's Accounts" of the Parish Church.[36] W. F. Atkinson, a local solicitor, provided him with "an old memorandum book kept by the Rev. W. Atkinson" which, as Scruton remarked:

"contains many interesting notes, interspersed with several rough sketches of local scenes from the pencil of that reverend Gentleman".[37]

James Hartley, the school teacher, "whose useful little book was printed in 1776"[38] provided Scruton with details of the Bradford Boar Legend and other local traditions.

Being an active Nonconformist himself Scruton was aware of, and had access to, the main sources for the history of Bradford Dissent. Useful primary sources on this subject used by Scruton included the Quaker Burial and Death Registers of 1652; the minutes of numerous Methodist, Baptist and other local Chapels, and the "Private Memoirs of E[sther]. & B[enjamin]. Seebohm", (edited by their sons, Frederick, Henry and Benjamin) which, as Scruton states, is "a delightful addition to the annals of Quaker biography".[39] Unsurprisingly throughout the *Pen and Pencil Pictures* references appear to William W. Stamp's book on *Methodism in Bradford* (1841); the *Diary of Oliver Heywood* edited by Horsfall Turner and J. G. Miall's celebrated *History of Congregationalism in Yorkshire*.

Throughout his working life, Scruton, having access to various manuscript collections, and utilising the resources available to him at the office of the *Bradford Observer* and the solicitor's firm where he worked, collected a considerable amount of historical material – newspaper cuttings, photographs, letters, pamphlets, autographed books and other ephemera. Using such material Scruton made detailed notes on wide and varied subjects: the "family names in the West-Riding"; "The growth of the worsted trade in Bradford"; "ancient Bingley, Eccleshill, Horton"; "Bradford Streets forty years ago" and "Bradford in the Olden Times". Much of this material he collated and placed in well organised, and neatly presented scrapbooks.[40]

These scrapbooks (about fourteen in total), are beautifully bound, each measuring about 12 inches by ten and titled in embossed lettering. They contain information on many leading figures of the day, some local celebrities, and other important national figures with links to Bradford. Leaflets and newspaper cuttings appear on the novelists' Charlotte Brontë and Charles Dickens; the caricaturist George Cruikshank, John Sharp, Archbishop of York; Abraham Sharp of Horton Old Hall, Herbert J. Gladstone, MP for Leeds and son of the Prime Minister; and W. E. Forster, MP for Bradford. Notes are found, some printed others in Scruton's legible but spidery hand-writing on John James, author of *'History of Bradford'*, John Nicholson, 'The Airedale Poet'; the poets Ben Preston and Abraham Holroyd; Sir Titus Salt,[41] Samuel Cunliffe Lister, textile manufacturer, Richard Oastler, factory reformer, Edward Baines, Count Zinzendorf, founder of the Moravian Movement; Captain James Cook, explorer, and many more significant figures too numerous to list.[42]

Much of the material contained in these scrapbooks Scruton used as separate chapters, or as sections in his *Pen and Pencil*

Pictures of Old Bradford. On his death in 1924 the scrapbooks were divided up, some going to private collectors while other parts were obtained by the local library in Bradford. Today, the bulk of Scruton's Scrapbooks can be seen at the West Yorkshire Archives, the Margaret McMillan Building, Bradford.

The Index: house-style and explanatory notes

Unlike earlier indexes of Scruton's *Pen and Pencil Pictures* which list surnames of people only, this index is fully comprehensive including place-names, subjects, and themes as well as surnames. As such, it should prove to be an indispensable tool for local and national historians using Scruton's book to explore Bradford's fascinating history.

This index is based on the standard version of Scruton's book as published by Thomas Brear of Bradford in 1889. The index is also compatible with the version of the book published by Mountain Press, Queensbury, in 1968, as they faithfully printed a facsimile of the 1889 text. Similarly, *The Amethyst Press*, Otley, in 1985 published an exact copy of the original adding a brief introduction by Jack Reynolds and a list of those who subscribed to the first publication of the book in 1889.

The house-style adopted in compiling this Index mainly follows that as laid out in the Chicago Writing Manual, widely used in universities, libraries and academic research generally. Entries are in alphabetical order based on the letter-by-letter arrangement, where the number of words in the entry heading is irrelevant. In following this arrangement the ampersand is taken as "and", and as such affects the alphabetical order of entries. "St" as in "St Augustine" is to be understood as an abbreviation for the noun "saint" fitting into the Index in that alphabetical order. Italics are used for publications (books, Journals and newspapers), and certain proper nouns such as the names of ships and Acts of Parliament.

The reader should be aware of other details. Where appropriate a short note is given explaining an entry, especially when identical names appear more than once. Places are given their locality. Many entries for a person contain the person's religious affiliation, i.e., Anglican, Baptist etc, and/or their occupation. Of course, place names change over time. Whenever this occurs in the text the reader is made aware of the change or variant in brackets after the entry name. For example, the user of the Index will be made aware that Bolling in Bradford is also known as Bowling and, in the Medieval period, Bolyng. Unless otherwise stated Churches, places, streets etc are in Bradford. Dates in entries are in brackets so as not to confuse them with page numbers

The Old Theatre Royal.

Illustrations & lists given by Scruton in his Pen & Pencil Pictures

Scene on the Bradford Canal .... Frontispiece
Bierley Hall, engraving by J. C. Bentley
Birthplace of "Prophet" John Wroe .... Title page
Lord Cranbrook .... Dedication
Two page Plan of Bradford 1800
Poll Tax list for Bradford (Bradeforth) .... Page 11
Poll Tax List for Manningham (Manygham) 12
Parish Church steeple hung with wool-packs 15
"Pity poor Bradford": The Bolling Hall Ghost 18
The first Bradford Factory: "The Holme" 19
Parish Church, middle of last century 20
Old Gateway: Unitarian Chapel 22
Parish Church in the time of Vicar Crosse 23
Parish Church before Restoration 25
Old pulpit-Parish Church 26
Parish Church after Restoration 27
Old Vicarage, Church Bank 27
Parish Church and Vicarage in 1810 28
Rev. John Crosse 32
Rev. Dr. W. Scoresby 35
Catalogue of the Vicars of Bradford 38
Old Christ Church, Darley Street 39
Items from an old account book 41
Old St. John's, Manchester Road 43
Old St. Mary's, Stott Hill 45
Old Unitarian Chapel 46
List of expenditure on Chapel Lane Chapel 48
Rev. Joseph Dawson 50
Rev. Nicholas T. Heineken 51
Quaker Chapel, Goodman's End 55
John Nelson in the Bradford Dungeon 57
The Old Cock-pit 58
Octagon Chapel, Horton Road 60
Old Sion Chapel, Bridge Street 66
Rev. Dr. Benjamin Godwin 67
Horton Lane Chapel, and Minister's House 71
Rev. Jonathan Glyde, ... 73
Wesley preaching from the steps of the Old Cock-pit 76

The Old Grammar School	79
The Old Mechanics' Institute, Leeds Road	85
List of the first disbursements of Bradford Library	94
List of book titles and sundries for the Library	95
The original Airedale College	98
Airedale College, Undercliffe	100
Baptist College, Horton,	101
Back of the Old Paper Hall	108
Toll Booth and old Shops, Ivegate	109
The old Justice Court	110
The Old Workhouse, Barkerend	113
The Old Piece Hall	114
The Old Market Building	119
The Old Market Cross	120
The Old Dispensary, High Street	123
The Old Theatre Royal	135
Mr Nunn as Jeremy Diddler	138
Miss Maria B. Jones, actress	142
Mr J. D. Stoyle as "Prince Paul"	144
The last of "The Old Royal"	148
Charles Rice as "Rip Van Winkle"	149
The Odd-Fellows' Hall	150
Old Post Office, Miller-gate	152
John Hudson	154
Union Passage	154
First list of Box Holders 1836	155
Old Bradford Bank	157
The Old Bank, Kirkgate	158
Wentworth & Co's Branch Bank, Market Street	160
The Wool Packs Inn,	165
List of hotels, Inns and taverns in 1822 and by whom kept	165
Back of the Church Steps Inn	166
Bull's Head Inn	169
The Old Sun Hotel	170
The Old Talbot Hotel	171
The Hope and Anchor Inn	172
Angus Holden, Mayor of Bradford	173
The White Swan Inn	173
Three Horse Shoes Inn	173
The Bee Hive Inn, Westgate	175
Spink-well Toll Bar	176
Old Bowling Green Hotel	178
John Hardy, MP	179
E. Cunliffe Lister, MP	181

Sir Titus Salt, Bart	192
The Right Hon. W. E. Forster, MP	195
Ripley's Dyeworks 1807	197
List of Bradford's Parliamentary Elections	198
Col. T. Perronet Thompson, MP	199
List of names possessing armorial bearings 1798	201
The Old Paper Hall	202
Stott hill House	203
Old doorway, Manor Hall	204
The Manor Hall, Kirkgate	205
Mr. John Rand	206
Rev. William Atkinson MA	207
Rev. David Clarkson, BD	209
Benjamin Seebohm	215
Sir Titus Salt's birthplace	215
S. Cunliffe Lister Esq. JP, DL	217
Horton Hall	217
Bolling Hall	218
Broadstones	223
Kirkgate in 1827	224
Old Shops – Bottom of Kirkgate	225
Mr. Manoah Rhodes' Old Shop	225
Old Shops in Westgate	226
Old Ivegate	227
Ald. Henry Brown	227
Brown and Muff's old Shop	228
Horse Fair in Bridge Street	229
Old Foundry, Tyrrel Street	230
Doorway of Old Corn (Soke) Mill	232
Old Shops in Westgate	235
W. Byles, Esq,	237
Birthplace of John Nicholson	238
Abraham Holroyd	239
William Overend Geller	241
Prophet Wroe	245
Thomas Ramsden	248
Blind jimmy	249

INDEX

Abbott, family, actors, 128
Abolition of flogging in the army, 182
Abolition of slavery, see Slave-trade Question
Abolition of stamp duty on newspapers, 182
Abolition of taxes in industry, 183
Abolition of the death sentence, 182
Abraham Bower & Co., 157
Ackroyd, George, local poet, 89, 160-161, 239
Ackroyd, John, poet, 239
Ackroyd, Messrs, post office box-holder, 155
Ackroyd, William, post office box-holder, 155
Ackworth, Dr., Baptist, 67, 88, 102
Ackworth, Quaker School, 211
Act of Uniformity 1662, 31, 47, 71, 209
Addams, Mr., R., lecturer, 92
Addingham, village 16 miles north of Bradford, 180, Farfield Hall 186
Addison, W. B., 89
Addison & Roper, 155
Addle, see Adel
Adel, (Addle), near Leeds, 47, 48, 208
Advertisement duty, on newspapers, 235
Adwalton, Leeds, 3, John Nelson preaches at 57
Adwalton Moor, battle of, 16
Aeschylius, ancient Greek dramatist, 127
Aire-dale, 13, 15
Airedale College, 73, 97-101, picture of the original Airedale College 98, illustration of Airedale College, Undercliffe 100
Aire, River, 13
Aked, family, 169
Aked, J. & T., 156
Aked, John, list of expenditure (1719), 48
Aked, John, 48, 94, 95, 113
Aked, Mr., senior constable, 113
Aked, Thomas, 236
Albert, Prince, husband of Queen Victoria, 146
Albion Court, 85, 88, 95
Albion Hotel, Ivegate, 174
Aldermanbury, district of Bradford, 58, 148
Ale-taster, 164
Alexander, William, his *History of Women*, 95
Alexandra Hotel, Bradford, 59, 216
Alfred, King, 3
Allerton, 12, 29, 44, Quakers at 52, 54,
Allerton-cum-Wilsden, 201
Allison, Mr., boot-maker, 227
Allott, Mr., watchmaker, 225
All Saints' Church, 44, 93
All Saints' Church, Warham, Norfolk, 207
Alpaca, 215, 216
America, 67, 68, 190, 214
Anacreontic, the, Lodge of the Independent Order of Odd Fellows, 150
Ancient Britons, 1, 2, 3
Anderson, J., Wilson, artist, 129, 130, 171, 240, 243, painting of "The Royal Oak" 243
Anderson, Professor, the "wizard of the North", strolling player, 132
Anderson, William, artist, 171
Anderton, Mrs., sister to Mr., John Wood, 207
Anderton, Swithin, Post office box-Holder, 155
Angel, The, Inn, Westgate, 165
Anne, Queen, 152
Anti-Corn Law League, 183, 206
Antinomianism, 32, 74
Anti-slavery, see Slavery
Apperley Bridge, 154, 171-172, 176

33

Appleton, photographer, Preface xi, xii
"Arab", HMS, 137
Aram, Eugene, theatrical play, 134
Archbishop of Canterbury, Lord, John, 27
Archbishop of York, 27, 35, 38, 82, 217
Arctic, the, 34, 35
Arianism, doctrine of, 32
Armada, Spanish, 1
Arminianism, (Scruton incorrectly writes "Armenian"), 32, 40, 64, General Baptists 68
Armstrong's Hotel, Horton Lane, 102, 243
Arnold, Dr., Thomas, of Rugby School, 195
Arnold, Jane, Martha, wife of W. E. Forster, 195
Art Journal, 242
Arthur, Miss, 41
Ashfield Terrace, Horton Road, 171
Aspinall, George, Swedenborgian, 75
Assize of Bread and Beer, 5
Astrology, 244
Atheism, 66, 67, 151
Athenaum, 236
Atherton, Rev., William, Methodist minister, 61
Atkinson, Mary, wife of Rev. William Atkinson, 208
Atkinson, Rev., Christopher, father of Rev., William Atkinson, 207
Atkinson, Rev., William, 81, 97, 103, *Memorandum* Book and sketch of the Bradford Bank 157, afternoon lecturer at the parish Church 207, picture of between pages 206-207, 208, dislike of Dissenters 208, pamphlets 208, known as "The Old Enquirer" 208, "The Looking Glass", series of tracts against Dissent 208, 230, 231, mention of portrait by W. O. Geller 241

Atkinson, W. F., solicitor, 157, 208
Australia, 36, 145
Auty, Mr., Squire, publisher, 235
Ayell, Willelmus, Medieval Poll Tax list, 11

Bacon, Mrs., of Idle, philanthropist, 100, 124, 205
Bacup, Rossendale in Lancashire, 62
Baildon, 207
Bailey & Holdsworth, tobacconists, In Broadstones, 225
Baines, Dr., P. A, 46
Baines, Edward, Jnr., 88, 195
Baines, Rev., Dr., bishop of Thespia, 45, 46
Bakes, Thomas, Innkeeper, 151
Baldock, Reginald de, Catalogue of vicars at Bradford 38
Baldock, Robert, Catalogue of vicars at Bradford 38
Baldwyn, Rev., Edward, Grammar School Master, 34, 81
Baldwyn, Rev., W, 97
Balfour, Mrs., Clara, Lucas, author and Temperance campaigner, 88
Balie, Thomas, priest in Bradford (1527), 28
Ballad of Flodden Field, 220
Ballot Act, 111, 112
Balme, Abraham, 27
Balme, family of, 8
Balme, John, 101
Balme, Miss, 124
Balme, Mr., original member of Horton Lane Independent Chapel, 69
Bandmann, Herr, actor, 149
Banke, Thomas, presbyter, Catalogue of Bradford vicars 38
Bankfoot, 43
Banks, George, of Leeds, politician, 179, 180, 181, 198
Banks, in Bradford, 156-162, picture of the old Bradford Bank 157

Banks, Thomas, presbyter of Bradford (1401), Catalogue of Bradford vicars 38
Bank Street, 119, 152, 153, 154, 157, 161, 162, The Fleece Inn 165, Hope & Anchor Inn, 165, 171, "Bob" Waterhouse's house in 185, 228
Bannockburn (1314), battle of, 10,
Baptism, practice of, 65
Baptist College, Bury, 67
Baptist College, Horton see Horton Baptist College
Baptists, the, 21, 58, 62-68, 104-5.
Barber, Rev., John, 89
Bardsley, Rev., Canon, Joseph, 37, 38
Barkerend, 8, 16, 20, 69, 80, 112, old workhouse 114, 223
Barkerend Road, 80
Barker, Joseph, 247
Barker, Ricardus, Medieval Poll Tax List 11
Barmby, James, Rev., 81
"Barnard's Survey", (1577), 205
Barnsley, South Yorkshire, 233
Barnwell, George, 129, 134
Baron, Rev., Benjamin, vicar of Bradford (1698-1706), Catalogue of Bradford vicars 38
Barr, Robert, 89
Barrett, Judy, spice-shop, 226, 248-249
Bartle, confectioner, 228
"Bartle's corner", 119, 127
Bartlett, Benjamin, apothecary, early Quaker, 2, 53, 210-212, married Elizabeth 210
Bartlett, Benjamin, Jnr., only child born to Benjamin and Elizabeth Bartlett, 210-212
Bartlett, Bradford cricketer, 171-172
Bartlett, Elizabeth, daughter of Joshua and Sarah Bartlett, wife of Henry Gurney, 210, 212
Bartlett, Elizabeth, wife of Benjamin Bartlett, 210

Bartlett, family, 210
Bartlett House, see Bolton Banks Farm
Bartlett, Joshua, yeoman, 210
Bateman & Sons, firm of, 155
Bateman, Mary, alleged witch, 244
Batley, town in Kirklees, south of Leeds, 12, 48
Battle of Hastings, 4
Baxter, Joseph, landlord of the Bowling Green Inn, 167
Baxter, Richard, Puritan divine, 210
Baxter, William, landlord, Royal Oak, 165
Bayley, Rev., Dr., Swedenborgian, 75
Beaconhill, 38
Beaconshaw, Gilbert, presbyter of Bradford (1503), 38
Beaumont, Dr., Thomas, 88, 92
Beaumont, Mr., 31, 92
Beaumont, writer, 130
Beccaria, Cesare, Italian criminologist, 95
Beckett & Co., Bank, 158
Bedford, gaol, 214
Beecroft, Mr., Tory candidate at Leeds, 195
Bee Hive Inn, Westgate, (formerly the Horse and Groom), 165, 174, picture of between 174-175
Behrens, Jacob, Sir, 92, 155
Belcher, Mr., Sun Hotel, 170
Belford, William, actor, 136, 144
Bell Chapel see Old Bell Chapel
Bell, Dr., Philosophical Society, 92
Bell, John, landlord of the Lord Nelson Inn, 165
Bell, Maggie, landlady of the Fox & Hounds Inn, 165
Bell-ringing, 167
Bentham, Jeremy, 188
Bentley, Abraham, town-crier & newsagent, 228
Bentley, family, 112
Bentley, Greenwood, solicitor, father of J. C. Bentley, 240, 241

Bentley, John, Bradford library, 97, 156
Bentley, Joseph Clayton, engraver & artist, son of Greenwood Bentley, 222, 240, 241, contribution to *Gems of European Art* 242, engravings "The Fountain", "The Sunny Day", and paintings "The Wooden Bridge", "The Book by the Way", "The Valley Farm", "The Way to Church", and "The Windmill" 242, 243
Bermondsey (area in Bradford between Cheapside and the Midland Railway), 174
Bermondsey Hotel, (later The London), 7, 138, 174
Berthon, John, of the Isle of Wight, 42
Berwickshire, south-east Scotland, 97
Bessingby, near Bridlington, 35
Bible Christians, 76
Bible Society, 46, 213
Bickerdike, Rev., J., 89
Bierley, 3, 52 (the Quakers), 69, 111, North Bierley 113, 201, Dr Richardson 222
Bierley Chapel, 69, 124
Bierley Hall, Picture of frontispiece, 3, 82, 212, 218, 222, 242
Bilton & Maud, grocers, 226
Bilton, James, Quaker, 113, 213
Bilton, John, Quaker, 113, 213
Bilton, Quaker family, 54
Bingley, 14, 73, 161
Birkbeck, Mr., of the Craven Bank, Settle, 157
Birkby, Esther, early Quaker, 52
Birkenshaw, 50, 80
Birstall, village south of Bradford-Leeds, John Nelson from 57, 64, 249
Bishop Blaize Festivals, 122, 167
Bishop Blaize Inn, Kirkgate, 165
Bishop of Ripon, 43
Black Abbey, 111

"Black book of Sinecures and Pensions of British Government", by Squire Auty, 235
Blackburn, Bailey, druggist, 225
Blackburn, John & Son, printers, later William Howgill Blackburn, 234
Blackburn, town in Lancashire, 9
Blackburn, William Howgill, printer & music dealer, 227, 234
Blackburnshire, Hundred of Blackburn, Lancashire, 7
Black Death, 11, plague of (1665) 19
Blackie, Prof., 122
Blackstone, Sir, William, Judge and Tory politician, His commentaries 95
Blaize, bishop, 122, 130, bishop Blaize Festivals 167
Blaize, bishop, Inn, Kirkgate, 165
Blamires, Joe, landlord of the Boar's Head Inn, 174
Blanche, daughter of Henry, Duke of Lancaster, 9
Blanket, Thomas, of Bristol, 77
Blazeby, Billy, blind musician, 250
Blazet, Rev., 31, 38
Bleazards, Quaker family, 54
"Blind Jimmy", name given to James Mortimer, 249, picture of between pages 248-249
"Blind Sam", 250
Bloomsbury Chapel (Baptist), London, 68
"Blue Book of British Manufactures" (1848), by Squire Auty, 235
Board Schools, 105, 107
Boar Legend, 9-10, 77
Boar's Head Inn, Market Street, 165, 174, 228
Boar's Well, see Boar Legend
"Bob" Waterhouse's, Bank Street, 185
Boddington, Rev., J. C, 89

Boissermas, 155
Boldshay, house near Miryshaw, Bradford, Etymology of the name 205
Bollans, , Rev.,Thomas, 27
Bolling, see Bowling
Bolling, family, 219
Bolling, foundry, 5
Bolling Hall, siege of Bradford 16, 24, 7, 201, 218, picture of between pages 218-219, description of 218, 219, 221, 222
Bolling Hall Ghost, 17, illustration of 18
Bolling, Robert de, 219
Bolling, Rosamond, later wife of Richard Tempest, 219, 221
Bolling, Tristram, 219
Bolling, William de, 219
Bolton, region of Bradford (not to be confused with Bolton, Lancashire), 13, 195, 211, 212
Bolton Banks Farm, (AKA Walnut House and Bartlett House), 211
Bolton House, home of the Hustler family, 55, 56, 91, 195
Bolton Lane, 211
Bolton Road, 81, 104, 166, 203
Bonas, Abednego, early Quaker, 52
Bonas, Croysdill, early Quaker, 52
Bond Street, 58
Bonnell, John, 113
Booth, Mr., organ tuner, 41
Booth, Congregational Church, 70
Booth Street, 89
Boroughbridge, North Yorkshire, 10
Borough West Schools, 72, 107
Borries, Julia, von, mother of Benjamin Seebohm, 214
Boswell, James, his *Corsica*, 95
Botham, Joseph, Sheffield based Architect, 61
Bottomley, Mr., photographer, Preface xi,
Bournemouth, Dorset, 37
Bower, Abraham, 157

Bower, family, 202, 205
Bower, Jeremiah, 210
Bower, Jeremy, Landlord, tanner & barber, 164
Bower, Miss, 97
Bower, Rosamond, wife of Jeremiah Bower, 210
Bowland Street, 76
Bowling (Bolling or Bollyng), 12, 13, 20, 43, 44, 52, early school at 106,111,113, 201, 218, 220, Manor of 222, birthplace of prophet John Wroe 245
Bowling Congregational Church, 73
Bowling Green, 64, 168, 177, 229
Bowling Green Hotel, Bridge Street, 20, 152, 153, 165, 167, 168, 175, 177, illustration of 178, 181, headquarters of the Liberals 188, 235
Bowling Green Inn, 167, 168, 235
Bowling Iron Works, 5, 160, 218, 222
Bowling, John, printer of Leeds, 12, 94, 96
Bowling Lane, see Manchester Road
Bowron, Joshua, landlord, White Lion Inn 166
Boy & Barrel Inn, Westgate, 165
Boyle, Captain, 137
Bracewell, near Skipton, 219, 220
Bradford Antiquary, Preface xi, footnote 164
Bradford Artists' Society of Painting and Sculpture, 240
Bradford & Wakefield Chronicle, 236
Bradford Bank, 156, 157
Bradford Banking Co., 155, 159, 160, 161
Bradford Beck, 2-3, 20, 79, 111, 168
Bradford Canal, Illustration, frontispiece, 19, 94, 212
Bradford Church Building Society, 44

Bradford Church Institute, see Church Institute
Bradford Club, 168
Bradford Commercial Bank, (originally The Bradford Commercial Joint Stock Banking Co.,), 161
Bradford Commercial Joint Stock Banking Co., 161
Bradford Conservative Club, 187
Bradford Courier, 110-111, 113, 119, 121, 124, 153, Bradford Banking Company 159, originally known as the *Bradford Courier and West Riding Advertiser* 235, 236, 240
Bradford Cricket Club, 171
Bradford Daily Telegraph, 161, 235, 237, see also under Thomas Shields and Newspapers
Bradford Directory, 235
Bradford District Bank, 161
Bradford, etymology of name 2
Bradford Fair, 125
Bradford Florist Society, 169
Bradford Gas Company, 42
Bradford Grammar School, for boys, 50, 64, 76, 77-83, illustration of the old school 79, Joseph Watson, second master 156, old Grammar School 167, attended by Henry Wickham 190, 209, 222, 237
Bradford Grammar School, for girls, 83
Bradford Historical & Antiquarian Society, Preface xii, 108
Bradfordian, The, journal of Bradford Grammar School, 83
Bradfordian, The, magazine published by Abraham Holroyd, 238, 239
Bradford Infirmary, 42, 91, 122, 123, 124, 125, 163, see also under Fever Hospital, Eye and Ear Hospital, Institute for the Blind, Children's Hospital, and Convalescent Homes
Bradford, John, Landlord of White Swan Inn and a coachman, 166, 172, 177
Bradford Law Institute, 85
Bradford Library, 94, 96-97, 160
Bradford Long-pledged Teetotal Association, 107
Bradford Market, 105, 247
Bradford Mechanic's Institute, see Mechanics Institute
Bradford Moor, 16, 172
Bradford, Mrs., librarian of the Subscription library, 96
Bradford Observer, Preface xii, 153, 236, first issued as a daily paper 237
Bradford Old Bank, 155
Bradford Parish Church, see Church, Parish
Bradford Rectory, 205
Bradford Review, 239
Bradford School Board, 240
Bradford Subscription Library, 50, 69, 93-97, 123
Bradford Theatre Royal, 130
Bradford Times, 190
Bradford Town Mission, see Town Mission
Bradford Tradesmen's Benevolent Society, 248
Bradford Union, the, 113, 114
Bradgate, Rev., Ferrand, vicar of Bradford (1706-1710), 38
Bradpole, Dorsetshire, birthplace of W. E. Forster, 195
Brady, Dr., Philosophical Society, 92
Braithwaite, John, Preface xii
Brandard, Mr., of London, engraver, tutor of J. C. Bentley, 241
Branwell, Maria, wife of Patrick Brontë, 40, 41
Branwell, Mr., T., 40, 41
Branxton Moor, battle of, 220
Bray, Dr., His library 89
Brear, Mr., shopkeeper, Broadstones,

224
Brereton, John Le Gay, poet, 239
Brewster, Sir, David, 91
Bridges, Dr., 92
Bridge Street, 20, 62, 165, 167, disturbances at the 1867 election 196, 229, picture of Horse Fair in Bridge Street 229, 244
Brigantes, Celtic tribe, Yorkshire, 1-2
Briggs, Arthur, 93
Brighouse Monthly Meeting, Quaker, 214
Bright, John, politician, 163, 191
Bristol, port of, 77, 149
Britannia Inn, Market Street, 165, 174
Britannia Theatre, London, 149
Britons, ancient see Ancient Britons
Britton, Mr., post office box-holder, 156
British Institution, London, 241
Broadbent & Son, James, 155
Broadley, Samuel, Baptist benefactor, 102, 124
Broad-stones, 3, 20, 50, 80, picture of between pages 222 and 223, 223, 224, Mr., Spencer, printer 234
Brontë, Charlotte, Title page, 40, 234, 237
Brontë, family, 237
Brontë, Patrick Branwell, 171, 243, mention of his paintings of Rev., William Morgan and Rev Henry Heap 243
Brontë, Rev., Patrick, 40, 41, 97, "The Maid of Killarney" and "The Cottage in the Wood" 234, 237, 243
Brontë sisters, 237
Brooke, Bond & Co., 225
Brooke, Gustavus Vaughan, actor, 129, 145, 147
Brooksbank, Abraham, 38
Brooksbank, William, silversmith, 227

Brougham, Lord, 118, 163
Brown & Muff, shop, 20
Brown Cow Inn, Kirkgate, 165, 225, 245
"Brown Cow Shop", owned by Messrs Watson, Broadstones, 225
Brown, George, 120, 152
Brown, Henry, Alderman, 82, 86, 227, picture of 227, 228, picture of Brown & Muffs old shop 228
Brown, John, Wesleyan, 103
Brown, Mrs., mother of Henry, 227-228
Brownroyd Hill, Wibsey, 74
Brumfit, Abraham, 155
Brumfit & Simpson, tallow chandlers, 226
Brumfit, tailor and pawnbroker, 225
Brunswick Place, 208
Buckstone, Mr., J. B., co-lessee of the Alexandra Theatre, 149
Bull-baiting, 168
Bull, Parson, G, S, of Bierley, 42, 156
Buller and wife, (1677), 38
Buller, Francis, 38
Bull-ring, 168
Bull's Head Inn, Westgate, 165, 168, 169, illustration of 169, 226, 243
Bulton, Willelmus de, Medieval Poll Tax list 11
Bunting, Corporal, 134
Bunting, Rev., Dr., Jabez, most prominent Wesleyan Methodist after Wesley's death (1791), 61, 134
Bunyan, John, 214
Burdsall, "Dickey", preacher, 249
Burfield, , Rev., Canon, 42
Burgage-houses, 7, 200
Burges, Johannes, Medieval Poll Tax list 12
Burgesses, 6, 7
Burges, Wilhelmus, Medieval Poll Tax list 11

Burnaby, presumably Scruton is Referring to Colonel Frederick Gustavus Burnaby, 163
Burnet, Rev., Dr., John, 26, 36, 37, 38, 88, 89, 92-3,
Burnet Field, Little Horton, 64
Burritt, Elihu, American philanthropist and social activist, 87
Burton, Nicholas de, steward of Henry de Lacy, 5
Burton-on-Trent, Staffordshire, 204
Bury, Greater Manchester, formerly Lancashire, 67
Bury, James, of Pendle Hill, 101
Bury St Edmunds, Suffolk, 99
Subfield, Col., 19
Busfield, J, A, of Upwood, 89, 203
Busfield, William, of Upwood, MP, 184, 185, 186, 187, 188, 198
Busfield, William, (Ferrand of Harden), 184-185, 198
Bussey, Peter, Chartist, 182-183, "physical force" policy 185
Busy Brig Fields, Bolton, Bradford, 211
Butler, Rev., Dr., Benjamin, teacher at Bradford Grammar School and "lecturer" at the parish Church, 64, 80, 81, 82
Butter Cross, Westgate, 127, 168
Butterfield, Mr., Post office box-holder 156
Butter Market, see Old Butter Market
Buxton, Anna, mother of W. E. Forster, 195
Buxton, Sir, Thomas, Fowell, anti-slavery campaigner, and W. E. Forster's uncle, 195
Byles, Henry, brother of William, 225
Byles, William, proprietor *Bradford Observer,* brother of Henry, 92, 155, 225, 236-237, picture of between pages 236-237
Byngham, de, Robert, presbyter, 38
Bynglay, Johanna de, 12

Byron, H, J, actor, 149

Caesar, Julius, 1, 3
Calais, France, 214, 220
Calamancoes, pieces of cloth, 114
Calamy, Edmund, provided a list of ejected ministers under the Clarendon Code (160-1665), 31
Callcott, artist, 242
Calverley Hall, 180
Calverley, Sir William, 109
Calvin, John, 64, 241
Calvinism, 64, 68, 69
Cambridge, 35, 209
Campbell, Rev., Dr., James Robertson, Minister of Horton Lane Congregational Church, 72, 73, 92
Campbell, Thomas, poet, 241
Canal, 94, 174, 224, see also Bradford Canal and Leeds-Liverpool Canal,
Canal Company, 94
Canal Road, 174
"Canker-Mark", the duty levied on Four-penny stamps, 235
Capital punishment, 182
Captain Street, 203
Carausius, Roman emperor, 3
Cardinal Manning, English Cardinal and Archbishop of Westminster, 163
Carey, Rev., John, first minister of Little Horton Moravian Church, 74
Carey, Sarah Annie, poet, 239
Carlisle, Cumbria, 131
Carlyle, Mrs., 195
Carlyle, Thomas, 195
Carmelite Friars, of York, 29
Carr End, Wensleydale, 211
Carrington, Ben, postman, 152
Carter, Bennet, Preface xii
Castle, at Bradford, 7, 200
Cater, James, solicitor, 148
Catholic Apostolic Church, 76

Catholic emancipation, 180
Cattle Fair, 229
Cavendish, Lady, Frederick, 83
Cavendish, Sir, Frederick, 163
Cedar of Lebanon, 222
Census (1801), 19
Central Coffee Tavern, 210, 225
Chaloner, partner of Wentworth, Rishworth & Chaloner, Bankers, 159
Chamber of Commerce, 168
Channel Islands, 37
Chantry, confectioner, 227
Chapel, Chapel Green, 48
Chapel Court, Kirkgate, 96, 225
Chapel Fold, Wibsey, 48, 74
Chapel Green, Little Horton, 48, 68
Chapel Lane, 20, 45, 48, 49, 50, 69, Unitarian Chapel 205, 234
Chapel Lane Chapel, 48, 49-52, 69
Chapel of Ease, Thornton, 29
Chapel of St Sitha, 13, 37
Chapel Street, 106, Quaker School 212
"Charity sermons", 103
Charles I, King, 13, 24, 30, 38
Charles II, King, 19, 78
Charles Street, 117, 172
Charnley, Hugh, 205
Charter (1251), to hold a market, 119
Chartism, 36, 56, see Peter Bussey, William Martin 185, 186, see William Martin, the People's Charter 186, James Clarkson 186, George Julian Harney 190, William Martin 190, Thomas Cooper 195
Chartlett, Dr., Arthur, 82
Chatterton, Mrs., owner of a travelling theatre, 133, 134, 135
Chatterton, Mr., spice merchant, 226
Chatterton's, Theatre Company, 131, 133-134
Chaucer, Geoffrey, poet and author, Canterbury Tales 1

"Cheap-jacks", 229
Cheapside, 20, 40, 122, 148, 158, 175
Cheeseborough, William, (Scruton also spells it Cheesebrough), 86, post office box-holder 155
Cheesebrough, John, Post office box-holder 156
Cheetham, Mr., coach-builder, 205
Chellawe, Gilbertus, Medieval Poll Tax list 11
Chellow, Bradford, 219
Children's Hospital, 161, 163
Childs, Mr., Owner of School-room in Drewton Street 75
Chinese War, (Second Opium War 1856-1860), 191
Choral Society, 169
Chown, Rev., J. P., Baptist, Minister of Sion Baptist Church 67, visit to America 68, pastor at Bloomsbury Chapel, London 68, death 68, 88, 102, 125
Christ Church, Darley Street, 39-40, illustration of 39, 42, the verger's "listing shoes" 42, 42, 121, 124, 128, 229, 243
Christ Church, Eldon Place, Manningham Lane, 40, 42, 75
Christ Church School, 104
Christeal Abbey, see Kirkstall Abbey
Christian Knowledge Society, 89
Christmas "Waits", see Waits
Church Bank, The old vicarage 27, 96, 166, 223
Church-bridge, near Broad-stones, 20
Church Choral Society, 89
Church Hill, Bradford, 2
Church Institute (Institution), 36, 75, 85, 88, 160
Church Literary Institute, 88-90
Church of England, 75
Church, parish, St Peters (1281) 4, glebe land 6, first historical reference 7, 8, value in 1292 10, siege of during Civil War 14-16,

illustration of Church with woolsacks on tower 15, 20, illustration mid 19th century in between 20-21, 21, illustration of Church in the time of John Crosse 23, 23-28, illustration of before restoration between 24-25, illustration of Church after restoration between 26-27, illustration of the old vicarage 27, illustration of parish Church 1810 between pp 28-9, 39, 44, Wesley preached in, 60, 77, 113, 123, 157, Church bells ringing 179, 200, 201, glebe land 202, 203, Rev William Atkinson 207, Robert Clarkson 208, Joshua Bartlett pew rental 210, Robert de Bolling burial (219), 221, prophet John Wroe baptised at 245

Church rates, 35, 182

Church Steps, 80

Church Steps Inn, 166, illustration of the back of 166

Church Steps Society, 167

"City of Glasgow", ship lost at sea, 241

Civil Engineer, the, a Lodge of the Independent Order of Odd Fellows, 150

Civil War (1640s), 14-19, 23, 30, 47, 82, "Roundheads" 179, 209, Sharp family 217, 221, 222

Clapham, Rev., Thomas, 38, 80

Clare College, Cambridge, 209

Claridge, W., teacher Bradford Grammar School, 83

Clark, Charles Cowden, (Clarke), author, editor and literary critic, 88, 161

Clark, Rev., Henry, 42

Clarke, Mrs., supplied candles for the Church, 41

Clarke, Rev., Dr. Adam, Methodist preacher and theologian, three times President of the Wesleyan Methodist Conference, 61

Clarkson, James, solicitor, Chartist, 186

Clarkson, Mary, daughter of Robert Clarkson, wife of John Sharp, 209

Clarkson, Matthew, of New York, son of
David Clarkson, 209, 210

Clarkson, Mrs., David, 210

Clarkson, Rev., David, 82, 209-210, picture of between pages 208-209, published Works 210

Clarkson, Robert, seventeenth century Puritan, 208

Clarkson, William, son of Robert Clarkson, 208

Classifying inhabitants, Medieval System 7

Claxton, Marshall, artist, 241

Clay, Miss, library assistant, 96

Clayton, village near Bradford, 12, 32,

Clayton, Eunice, landlady, Horse Shoes Inn, wife of Jesse Clayton, 165, 173-174

Clayton, James, post office box-holder 156

Clayton, Jesse, shoe-smith and landlord of Three Horse Shoes Inn, 173

Clayton, Joseph, 171

Clayton, Joshua, Post office box-Holder 155

Clayton, T. & J., 155

Clayton, T. G., 86, 154-155

Clayton, William, Post office box-holder 156

Clemesha & Chantry, confectioners, 227

Clerk, Johannes, Medieval Poll Tax list 11

Cliffe Wood, Bradford, 9, 77

Clifford, Lord, of Skipton Castle, 219

Clough, Hannah, landlady of Bishop Blaize Inn, 165

Clough, Mr., teacher at the Mechanics Institute, 88

Clough, Robert, landlord, Unicorn Inn, 166
Clowes, Rev., F, Baptist, 67, 102
"Clubbing-up", system by which poor families group together to buy a weekly newspaper, 235-236
Coaches, 84, 175, 177, the "Royal-Mail"153, the "Heavy Coach" 153, the "Highfyer" coach 172, 177, the "Rockingham-Bob" Coach 175, The "Defiance" stage-coach 177, The "Duke of Leeds coach 177, "Royal Mail", stage-coach traffic 177, The "Courier" 177, The Union 177, the Leeds coach 214
Coach-men, 177
Coates, "Joe", singer, 174
Coates, William, post-master, 156, 185
Cobbett, William, 121
Cobden, Richard, Liberal politician and social reformer, 183, 191, 206
"Cock and Bottle" Inn, Barkerend, 16, 165
Cockin, Rev., Joseph, Congregationalist, 69
"Cockle-Jack", famous coachman., 177
Cock-pit, the first Methodist meeting place, Bradford, 57, 58, illustration of the Cock-pit, 58, 59, meeting place for the Baptists, 63, 64, 76, 111, 113, 126, service held by Prophet Wroe 244, 245
Cockshot, Mr., druggist, 225
"Cockshott's Corner", name given to Cockshott's shop on Godwin Street, 225
Coffey, Rev., R. S. minister of Infirmary Street Presbyterian Church, 74
Coleby Hall, Lincoln, Preface xii
Coleridge, Hartley, author of "Northern Worthies", 171
Coley, near Halifax, 14, 47

"College Chapel", Congregationalist, 73
College of Physicians, London, 211
College of the Blessed Mary, see Newark College
Collier, Rev., Dr., Laird, 52
Colne, near Pendle, Lancashire, 3
Columbia, University of, 67
Commercial Bank, Bradford, 155
Commercial Bank, Halifax, 162
Commercial Prosperity, 19
Commercial Street, 45
Commonwealth, the, Cromwell's rule, 1, 31, 78, 202
Communism, 88
Confessor, King Edward, 5
Congregationalism, (Independents), 21, 48, 68-73, 104, 182, Miall's "History of Congregationalism in Yorkshire" 239, see under Horton Lane Congregational Church
Congregational Magazine, 72
Congregational Union of England and Wales, 72
Coniston, Cumbria, residence of Rev., Dr., John Burnet, 37
Conqueror, William, the, 4, "William the Bastard" 4
Constable, John, artist, 242
Constantine, Roman emperor, 3
Convalescent Homes, 163
"Conway, Derwent", pseudonym of Henry D. Inglis, editor of *Bradford Courier,* 124, 240
Cook, Eliza, author, 147
Cooke, William, proprietor of the *Bradford Times,* 190
Cooper, orator, 151, 195
Cooper, Rev., James, vicar of St Judes, 43, 89
Cooper, Thomas, Chartist poet-orator, 195
Copeland, Mr., of Liverpool, 144
Cork & Bottle Inn, Barker-end, 165
Corker, Rev., Francis, 30, 31, 38
Corn Laws, and anti-Corn law

agitation, 168, 180, 183, T. P. Thompson's "Corn Law Catechism" 188, Titus Salt and 193, William Rand and 206
Cornwall, county of, 214
Corporation, the, 153, 154, 160, 229
Corrupt Practices Act, 195
Corunna, military incident at, 231
Cote, Johannes, Medieval Poll Tax List 11
Cotes, William de, presbyter, 38
Cottam, John, 208
Cottam, Mary, daughter of John, 208
Cottingley, village near Bradford, 189
Countess of Huntingdon, 57
"Courier", the, stage-coach, 177
Court Baron, 112
Court House, 91, 110, 111, 117, 182, 184, 190, 226, see also Old Court House
Courtland, squire, 134
Court of Requests, Darley Street, 112
Court Rolls, During reign of Henry VII, 109, 120, fourteenth century 164
"Courts Leet", 8, 109
Cousen, Charles, artist, brother of John Cousen, 222, 242
Cousen, John, artist & engraver, 242, plates include "Mercury & Herse*, "Towing the Victory into Gibraltar" and "The Morning after the Wreck" 242
Cousen, Mrs., draper, 227
Cousens, of Bradford, 156, 224
Cox, Dr., Baptist, 66
Crabtree, Rev., William, Baptist minister, 63, Westgate, 64, his Calvinism, 64, 65
Cragg, H. artist, Preface xii, 223
Cranbrook, Viscount, (Mr., Gathorne Hardy), Illustration of, unnumbered page at beginning of book, page before Preface, 40, 163, 180, 187, 198, 204, 207
Crane, Rev., John Lockwood, 81
Craven Bank, Ltd., Bradford, 162
Craven Bank, Settle, 157
Craven-dale, 10, 19
Craven, North Yorkshire, 10, 220
Creswick, artist, 242
Crimea, Ukraine, 146
Crocker, John, 49
Croft, Eliza, librarian of the Subscription Library, 96
Croft, John, 89, 92
Croft, Joseph, 161
Croft Street, Early school in 106
Cromwellbotham, Yorkshire, 221
Cromwell, Oliver, 52
Cromwell, Thomas, 220
"Cropper Lane", 208
Cropton, near Pickering, North Yorkshire, 34
Crosley, John, occupier of the Bowling Green, 167
Crosley, Rev., James, of Horton Lane Congregational Church, 70
Crosley, Thomas, 155, 167
Crosse, Hammond (1784), 38
Crosse, Rev., John, 24, 26, picture of, 28, 32-34, 38, 40, 41, took a service with Wesley 60, 81, 97, Sunday School work, 103, 104, 118, 165, 208
Crossley, Mr., Quaker tea-dealer, 226
Crosstones, near Todmorden, 32
Crousdale, Jeremy, early Quaker, 52
Cruikshank, George, caricaturist and book illustrator, 163
"crying the fair", custom of, 112
Cuckoo-bridge, Leeds Road, 20
Cuckson, Rev., John, 52
Cudworth, William, Preface xii, 217, his "Life and Correspondence of Abraham Sharp" 217
Cumberland, Earl of, 220, 221

Cunliffe, John of Addingham, father of E. C. Lister, 180
Cure, "Tommy", grocer & tallow chandler, 225
Curtays, Mageria, Medieval Poll Tax list 12
Cushman, sisters, both actresses, 136, 147
Cussons, bookseller, 226
Cuyp, Aelbert, artist, 242

Daisy Hill School, 106
Dale, George, hairdresser, 227
Dale, John, printer & stationer, 227
Dale Street, 91
Dalton, village near Huddersfield, 75
Dalton Society of the New Church, Swedenborgian, 75
Danes, invaders, 3
Darcy, Lord, 220
Darfield Street, 68
Darley Street, 10, 39, 40, 42, 96, 112, 123, 124, 133, 161, 229, 240, 246
Darlington, John, 91, 92, 113
Darney, William, Methodist lay preacher 58
Dartmouth, Devon, 204
Dawson, C, H, of Royd's Hall, 86, 91
Dawson, Christopher, son of Joseph Dawson, 50
Dawson, family, 218
Dawson, George, Nonconformist preacher and social activist, 88
Dawson, Jacob, eccentric local poet, 181
Dawson, Rev., Joseph, 47, 50, 51, picture of 50
Dawson, Joshua, early Quaker, 53
Dawson, Mary, daughter of Joseph Dawson, 50
Dawson, Nancy, 50
Dawson, Rachel, daughter of Joseph Dawson, 50

Dawson, William, ("Billy"), Methodist preacher, 61, 249
Dead Lane, 14, 28
Dean, Mr., 94, 95
Dean, Mr., S. E., Preface xii
Dean, Rev., John, Unitarian, 50, 69, 94, 95
Dearden, William, poet & author, 171, 239
De Bolling, Reginald, 38
De Bolling, Robert, 219
Décor, B. or Beaconhill, 38
Defiance, the, stage-coach, 177
De Frizinghall, Robert, 5
Deighton, Mr., dealer in fishing tackle, 228
de Lacy, see Lacy
Delf, 48
De Manygham, Dionisius, Medieval Poll Tax list 12
Deputy Lieutenant of the West Riding, 204
Derby, Lord, 191
Devonport, Plymouth, Devon, 185
Devonshire, county of, 71
Dewsbury, West Yorkshire, The Church at 7, 12, 15
Dickens, Charles, 107, 163, visit to Bradford 171
Dillenius, friend of Dr. Richardson, 222
Dillon, Charles, actor, 147, 149
Diocletian, Roman emperor, 3
Discount Bank, 160
Dis-establishment, 180, 191, 196
Disney, Rev., S, vicar of Halstead, 82
Dispensary, Bradford, 34, 96, 122, 123, picture of old dispensary 123, 124, 125, 133, contribution made by William Maud 213
Disraeli, Benjamin, politician, 191
Dissenters (Nonconformists), Chapter four, and 182, 196, 208
Dixon, Hepworth, author, editor, traveller, 87
Dobson, Elizabeth, widow of Allerton,

45

29
Dodge, Jack, blind musician, 250
Dodsley, Robert, poet, 95
Dog & Shovel Inn, Kirkgate, 165
Domesday Book, (1086), 2, 4, 219
Doncaster, South Yorkshire, 12, 29, 126, 175, 233
Dorsetshire, county of, 195
Douglas, William, of Ilkley, 148
Dover, Kent, 214
Dowson, Rev., Henry, Baptist, At Westgate, 67, president of Baptist College, Bury, 67, 68, 102, mention of Geller's portrait of Dowson 241
Drake, friend of Dr Richardson, 222
Dramshops, 174, 175
Drewton Street, 75
Druids, 1
Drury Lane Theatre, London, 142
Dublin Hospital, 146
Dublin, Ireland, 129, University of 186
Dublin, Trinity College, 36
Duchy Court, 77, 205
Duckit, Mrs., hostess of the first Bradford Club, 168
Dudley Hill, 3, prophet John Wroe 58, 244
Duffield, family, 218
Duffield, Francis, 97, claiming use of armorial bearings (1798) 201
Duffield Hall, (also known as "Town Hill House"), 218
Dugdale, William, his *Visitation" of Yorkshire* (1665), 201
Duggan, Mr., Alderman, 144
"Duke of Leeds", stage-coach, 177
Duke of Wellington Inn, High Street, 165
Duke Street, 93, 129, 135, 136, 137, 144, 148
"Dumb John", barber, 224
Dunn, Mrs., landlady of the Albion Hotel, 174
Dunnance, Kircudbright, Scotland, 188

Dunstan Hall, Burton-on-Trent, 204
Durham, 4
Dury, Theodore, Rev., of Keighley, 91-92
Dynghale, Willelmus, On Poll Tax list 11
Dyson, William, Swedenborgian, 75

Eagle, John, 97
Earl of Newcastle, see Newcastle, Earl of
Earl of Zetland, 163
Earls of Lancaster, 9
Eastbrook Chapel, Methodist, 46, 61-62, 249
Eastbrook House, 119, 158, 202
East Morley & Bradford Savings Bank, 162
Ebenezer Chapel, Methodist New Connexion, Horton Lane, 62
Eccles, J, H, poet, 239
Eccleshill, 38, 52, Quakers at 54, early school at, 106, 201
Eccleshill Hall, 201
Eccleshill, Stephen de, presbyter, 38
Eccleshill, William de, presbyter, 38
Eckhard, J. & C., post office box-holder, 155
Ecroyd, Benjamin, post office box-holder, 155
Eddowes, Rev., John, 43
Edinburgh, Scotland, 72, 97, James Nichol publisher 210, Dr Fothergill, Quaker apothecary, trained at, Edinburgh Castle 240
Edleston, Rev., R., of Leeds, Swedenborgian, 75
Education, Borough West Schools 72, Bradford Grammar School 77-83, the Mechanics Institute 83-88, Forster's Education Bill 84, "popular Education" 84, Forster's Education Act 86, 193, 240, see Parochial Schools, Church

Literary institute 88-90,
Philosophical Society 90-93,
Subvert the lower classes 103,
see Schools, Free Library,
Technical College
Edward I, King, 7
Edward II, King, 24
Edward III, King, 1, 77
Edward IV, King, 13, 219
Edward & Alexandra, Prince & Princess of Wales, Visit Bradford (1882), 90
Edward the Confessor, King, 5
Egbert, King, 1
Ejectment, the, see also Act of Uniformity (1662), 47
Eldon Place, 249
Election, (1830), 180
Election, (1832), 122, 179, 180-182, 198
Election, (1835), 111, 183, 198
Election, (1837), 184, 198
Election, (1841), 187, 185, 198
Election, (1847), 187, 188, 198
Election, (1852), 189, 190, 198
Election, (1857), 191, 198
Election, (1859), 191, 194, 198
Election, (1861), 194, 198
Election, (1865), 195, 198
Election, (1867), 196-197, 198
Election, (1868), 197, 198
Election, (1869), 197, 198
Election, (1874), 197, 198
Election, (1880), 197, 198
Election, (1885), 197, 199
Election, (1886), 197, 199
Elections, 179-184, see also Parliamentary elections
Eliot, George, novelist, 218
Elizabeth I, Queen, 7, 38, 78, 200, 205
Elland, near Halifax, West Yorkshire, 78
Ellis & Co., James, 123, 155
Ellis, James, Quaker, 113, 123, 213, 214, 231
Ellis, William, Post office box-holder 155
Elys, Johannes, On Poll Tax list 11
Elys, Thomas, Poll Tax list 12
Elys, Willelmus, Poll Tax list 12
Emmanuel & Son, 155
Emerson, Ralph Waldo, American writer, philosopher and abolitionist, 87
Empsall, T. T., Footnote 164
Endowed Schools, 83
Endowed Schools' Act, 78, 83
Endowed Schools Commissioners, 82
England, Abraham, preacher, Eastbrook Chapel, 249
Esholt, (sometimes spelt "Eshold"), seven miles north of Bradford, 48
Eure, Richard de, presbyter, 38
Evam, weaver of Gomersal, 5
Everingham, Robert de, Lord of the Heaton Manor, 5
Ewood Hall, Midgley near Halifax, 64, 101
Exchange & Discount Bank, 160
Exchange Rooms, 92, 96, 119, 120-122, 156, 160, 162, 163, 212
Exchange Station, 188
Exchange Street, 122
Exchange, The, Kirkgate, 91,
Exeter, Devon, 35
Exeter Hall, 146
Extension of the Franchise, 191, see also parliamentary elections
Eye and Ear Hospital, 163

Factories, appearance of 21, description of by Glyde 71, 114
Factory reform, 35, 218
Fairbairn, Rev., Dr., A. M., 101
Fairfax, Lady, wife of Sir Thomas, 16
Fairfax, Lord, Sir, Thomas, Siege of Bradford 14, 15, 16, 47, 208, 209, 222
Fair-gap, see Northgate

Fairlee, husband of Maria Jones, 143
Fairs, 6, see under Cattle fair, Horse Fair and Pleasure Fair
Fairweather Green, Bradford, 111, 171
Faith, The, a Lodge of the Independent Order of Odd-Fellows, 150
Faith, Hope and Charity, the, a Lodge of the Independent Order of Odd-Fellows, 150
Fakenham, Norfolk, 158
Faraday, Prof., 50-51, 91
Farfield Hall, Addingham, 186
Farnley Wood plot, (1663), 18, 210
Farrar, Henry, 85
Farrar, Jem, 133
Farrer, John, 103
Farrar, Joseph, Hatter, 228
Farrar, Joseph, secretary of Mechanic's Institute, 84, 85, 86
Farrar, Mr., tailor, 225
Faucit, Helen, actress, 136, 147
Fawcett, Canon of Low Moor, 24
Fawcett, Helen, actress, 136
Fawcett, "*Life of Oliver Heywood*", 48
Fawcett, Rev., Dr., John, Baptist preacher, 64, his *Commentary on the Bible*, and *Essay on Anger* 64, 82, 101, mention of portrait of Fawcett by Geller 241
Fawcett, Rev., Joshua, 88, 89, 91, title of lecture given at the philosophical society 91, 92, 155
Fawcett, Richard, 24, senior and junior, 104, 155, 216, 231
Fawcett, Stephen, author & poet, 239, "*Bradford Legends & other Poems*" 239, 247
"Fayre Gappe", later known as Northgate, Bradford, 208
Fearnley, Joshua, Post office box-holder, 155
Feast of St Andrew, 6
Feather, William, "rhyming shoemaker", 227
Fechter, dramatist, 163
Federer, Charles Antoine, Footnote reference to his "Ballad of Flodden Field" (1884) 220
Female Educational Institute, 107
Female Friendly Society, 213
Fennell, Jane, daughter of John, 40, 41
Fennell, John, Headmaster of Wesleyan Academy near Bradford, 40, 41
Ferdinando, Lord Fairfax, 208
Ferrand, Rev., Bradgate, vicar of Bradford (1706-10), 38
Ferrand, of St Ives, 203
Ferry-bridge, West Yorkshire, 175
Feudalism, 1, 5-12, 77, 200
Fever Hospital, Bradford, 68, 163
Ffabe, Johannes, Poll Tax list 12
Ffrisynghall, Adam, Poll Tax list 5, 12
Field, James, landlord Brittania Inn, 165
Field, John, of Shipley, 27
Field, Joshua, 97, claiming use of armorial bearings (1798) 201
Field of the Cloth of Gold, 220
Firth, James, Post office box-holder, 155
Fisher & Co., publishers, 242
Fison & Sons, firm of, 155
Fison, Mr., 195
Fitzgerald, Major, of Richmond, 205
Fitzgeralds, 205
Fitzwilliam, Mrs., actress, of the Haymarket, 147
Flaxman, sculptor, 27
Fleece Inn, Bank Street, 162, 165, 175
Fleet Prison, London, 222
Fletcher, Dick, coachman, 177
Fletcher, Jim, blind musician, 250
Fletcher, writer, 130
Flintoff, Jack, cricketer, 150, 171, landlord of Hope & Anchor Inn 172

Flodden Field, battle of, (also known as battle of Branxton Moor 1513), 220
"Flood-gates", Bradford, 224
Flower Show, (1827), 169-170
Forbes, Sir, Henry, 86, 153, 155, 189, *Bradford Observer* 236
Forrest, James, landlord of Hare & Hounds Inn, 165
Forrest, Mr., actor, 134
Forrest, Sylvester, landlord of the Hope & Anchor Inn, 165
Forrest, Tom, coachman, 177
Forster Square, 122, 152, 156, 223
Forster, W. E. MP, Preface xii, 82, 83, 84, 86, 87, lectures given at the Mechanics Institute 88, 105, 163, 188, 190, 194, picture of between pages 194-195, biographical note 195, 197, elected without contest (1861 and 1865) 199, Parliamentary Election (1868) 198, Election (1885) 199, 214,
Forster, William, father of W. E. Forster, Quaker, 195, 198, 214, "Memoirs of William Forster" by Benjamin Seebohm 214
Fortune-telling, John James refers to 244, John Hepworth 244, astrology 244
Foster, Joe, 174
Foster, John, of Hornby Castle, 174
Foster, John, of Queensbury, 116,
Foster, Mr., Baptist, 101
Foster's Buildings, 79
Fothergill, John, Quaker, 211
Fothergill, Dr., apothecary, Quaker, 211-212, friend of Dr. Richardson 222
Fountain Street, Quaker Meeting House 53, 55,
Four-penny stamp duty see "Canker-mark"
Fox & Hounds Inn, North Wing, 165
Fox, George, founder of the Quakers, 52, 53, 56

Fox, Mr., landlord of the White Swan, 172
France, architect, 161, 214
Frankelayn, Rev., William, 38
Frankfort, Germany, 214
Frankland, Elizabeth, Baptist residing in Manningham, 62
Franks, optician, 227
Fraser, Rev., Dr., 88, 101
Frechville, Sir, Peter, married Elizabeth Tempest, 221
Freckleton, Rev., T. W., 52
Free Court, 5, 8
Freeholders, of Bradford, 8
Free Library, also see Subscription Library, 107
Freemasons, 130
Free Methodist Church, Chapel in Bridge Street 62
Free-trade, 180, 188, 189, 206
French Revolutionary Wars, 19
Friedensthal, Germany, 214
Friendly Mechanic, The, a Lodge of the Independent Order of Odd-Fellows, 150
Friends' Provident Institution, 112, 212
Frizinghall, 5, 52 ("Phrizinghall")
Frizinghall, Robert de, 5
Frost, Rev., Joseph Loxdale, 43, 89
Fryer, Mrs., landlady of the Bowling Green, 167
Fulling Mill, 2
Fulneck, Moravian centre, Pudsey, 73
Furness, Cumbria, 79
Furniss, Harold, artist, Preface xii

Gainsborough, Lincolnshire, 30
Gainsborough, Thomas, artist, 242
Gale, Rev., Knight, 44
Gallows, at Bradford, 5
"Gallows Close", 5
Gamel, Lord of Manor in Domesday Book, 4
Game Laws, repeal of, 183

Gamble, John, Post office box-holder, 155
Game laws, repeal of, 183
Gardiner, Walter, solicitor, 161
Gardiner, Jeffery & Hardcastle, solicitors, 161
Garnett, Eleanor, wife of James, 69
Garnett, James, owner of the Paper Hall, Barkerend, 69, 70, 86, 202, 236
Garnett, Richard, 70
Garnett, R. J. & W., firm of, 155
Gascoigne, Mr., Sun Hotel, 170
Gascoigne, William, of Shipley, 221
Gas Company, see Bradford Gas Company
Gaskarth, Henry, shop-keeper, 201, 226, 234
Gaskell, G. A., artist, Preface xii
Gaskell, Mrs., Elizabeth, her "Life of Charlotte Brontë", 40, 41
Gate Toll, 8
Gaunt, John of, 9
Gaussez & Boissermas, 155
Gell, Thomas, 28
Geller, Angelina, local artist, Preface xii, 240
Geller, James, engraver, brother of W. O. Geller, 241
Geller, William Henry, artist, son of W. O. Geller, 241
Geller, William Overend, artist, father of Angelina Geller, 240-241, picture of between pages 240-241, painting of "Cymon and Iphigenia" 241, "Death bed of Calvin" 241, "Deathbed of Wesley" 241, portrait of Thomas Campbell 241, engraving titled "Franklin at the Court of France" 241, portraits of John Nicholson, Dr. Richardson, Rev Henry Heap, Rev N. T. Heineken, Rev W. Atkinson, Rev Thomas Taylor, Rev William Steadman, Rev Jonathan Glyde, Rev Henry Dowson and Dr John Fawcett 241, painting of the "Bull's Head" 243
Gellys, Dyonis, presbyter, 38
Gellys, Henry, presbyter, 38
General Baptists (Arminian), 68
General Quarter Sessions for the West Riding, 211
Geneva gown, Worn by Rev., William Atkinson 207
Gent, Thomas, 234
Gentleman's Magazine, 40, 59
George III, King, 64
George IV, King, 138
George Hotel, Market Street, 160, 171, 194
George, W., Post-box holder 155, 161
German Church, Liverpool, 76
German Emperor, 220
German Evangelical Church, 75-76
Germany, 214
Ghosts, see reference to Bolling Hall and the Paper Hall
Gibson, John, landlord of the White Horse Inn, 166
"gin palace", 175
Girlington, district of Bradford, 44
Gisburn, Lancashire, 110
Gissop, B, locksmith, 41
Gladstone, William, politician, 204
Glasgow, Scotland, 72, 74, 153
Glebe, Church land, 6
Globe, the, Lodge of the Independent Order of Odd-Fellows, 150
Glossop, William, Preface xii
Gloucester, town of, 103
Glyde, Rev., Jonathan, minister of Horton Lane Congregational Church, 71, 72, picture of opposite page 72, 88, 106-107, mention of Glyde's portrait by Geller 241
Godwin, J. V., son of Benjamin Godwin, 67, 84, 197, parliamentary election (1874) 198
Godwin, Rev., Dr., Benjamin, Baptist,

66, picture of opposite page 66, tutor at Horton College, 66, 67, "Lectures on Atheistic Controversy" 67, anti-slavery 67, 71, 84, 88, 102, 213, *Bradford Observer* 236
Godwin Street, 225
Goit, or Old Stream, 231
Golden Fleece, The, a Lodge of the Independent Order of Odd-Fellows, 150
Golden Lion, Leeds, 153
Gomersal, Kirklees, West Yorkshire, 5, 12
Good Intent, The, a Lodge of the Independent Order of Odd-Fellows, 150
Goodmansend, 20, 27, 28, 52, 53, 54, illustration of Quaker Chapel on 55, 66, bookshop of Dudley Rocket 94
Gornoszynski, I. F., lecturer at Philosophical Society 92
Gott, John, organist, 41
Gough, His book titled *Britannia* 9
Gravelines, Northern France, 220
Great Grimsby, Lincolnshire, 215
Great Horton, 10, 44, 74, 224
Grecian Theatre, London, 149
Green, Elizabeth, 210
Green, Eliza Craven, poetess, 239
Green, John, early Quaker, 53
Green, Mary, of Liversedge, 210
Green, Rev., S. G., Baptist, 92, 102
Green, Thomas, of Liversedge, 210
Green, Timy, landlord, Saracen's Head Inn, 165
Greenfield Congregational Church, Manningham, 73
Greenlay, Thomas, early member of Horton Lane Congregational Church, 70
Greenwood, F., Post office box-holder 155
Gregory, John, Scottish physician, his book titled *Comparative View*, 95

Grellet, Stephen, Quaker preacher, 214
Griffin Inn, The, 174
Grimshaw, Rev., William, perpetual curate of Haworth, friend of John Wesley, 32, 58, 59, 69, 168, 208
Grossmith, George, actor, singer, writer, 88
Grousdale, Jeremy, 52
Guildford, West Surrey, 37
Guiseley, Leeds, West Yorkshire, 40
Gurney, Henry, of Norwich, 210
Gwynne, elderly spinster in charge of the First Bradford Post Office, 152

Hadfield, George, of Manchester, 182, 183, parliamentary election (1835) 198
Haigh & Atkinson, 155, 156
Haigh & Light, firm of, 155
Haigh, George, Post office box-holder, 155, 156
Haigh, Thomas, secretary of the East Morley & Bradford Savings' Bank, 162
Hailstone, Edward, of Walton Hall, near Wakefield, 31, 37, 48, 171, 217
Hailstone, Samuel, lawyer, 84, 90, 155, 207, 217, 249
Hainsworth, Lewis, Preface xii
Hales, Edward, Presbyterian preacher, 69
Halifax, Calderdale, West Yorkshire, 12, 14, 15, 47, 57, 63, 64, 65, 73, 126, 153, 157, 162, 165, 171,177, 220, 223, 233
Halifax Theatre, 130
Hall, Mr., the cutler, 228
Hall, Rev., Robert, Baptist, 66, 79
Hallfield Chapel (Baptist), Manningham Lane, 68
Hallfield Road, 83

Hall Ings, 20, 62, 110, 117
Hall of Pleas, Ivegate, 109, 110, 226
Hall, Rev., Robert, schoolmaster, Bradford Grammar School, 79
Halstead, town in Essex, 82
Halton, de, Rev., Richard, 29, 38
Hamilton, actor, 139
Hammond, Thomas, Post office box-Holder 155
Hanson, Edmund, 99
Hanson, James, proprietor and editor of *Bradford Review*, 88, 92, 239
Hanson, Mrs., writer, wife of James Hanson, 239, "*Fanny Lee's Testimony*" 239, "*Poems & Social Tales*" 239
Hardacre, Ben, poet, 239
Hardaker, James, 197, parliamentary election (1874) 198
Hardcastle & Sons, 155
Hardcastle, Rev., Joshua, 50, 161
Hardcastle, William, Jnr., 157
Harden, village five miles north-west of Bradford, 184
Harding, 48
Hardy, Charles, brother of Lord Cranbrook, 40, 91, 180, 204
Hardy, family, 218
Hardy, Gathorne, see Cranbrook, Lord
Hardy, John, father of Lord Cranbrook, 40, 44, 86, 180, 184, 198, 204
Hardy, John, MP, elder brother of Lord Cranbrook, 86, 122, picture of 178, 179-180, 181, 182, 183, 184, 185, 198, 204
Hardy, Laurence, 218
Hardy, Mr., grandfather of Lord Cranbrook, 207
Hardy, post-box, 155
Hardy, Sir John, 44, 180
Hare & Hounds Inn, Westgate, 165
Harewood, West Yorkshire, 237
Hargreaves, Mr., confectioner, 225
Harker, William, of Pateley Bridge, 161
Harney, George, Julian, Chartist, 190
Harper, Willelmus, Poll Tax list 11
Harris, Alfred, 85, 89, 91, 92, 106, 158, 159, 191, 193, parliamentary election (1859) 198
Harris, Alfred, Jnr., 92, 158
Harris & Co., bank of, 158
Harris C. H. A., & Co., bank of, 158
Harris, Charles, 103, 106, 123, 157, 158, 159
Harris, H. A. & W. M., bank of, 158
Harris, Henry, 103, 121, 158, 159
Harris, Miss, 159
Harris, William Masterman, 158
Harrison, Mr., J. L., manager of the Yorkshire Banking Co., 161
Harrison, Mr., Sun Hotel, 170
Harris's Old Bank, 119
Harrying, of the North (1069), 4
Hartington, Lord, 163
Hartley, David, philosopher, 82
Hartley, James, schoolteacher, 9, 115
Hartley, Joshua, 48
Hartley, Rev., William, of Haworth, Baptist, 62
Hartshead-cum-Clifton, two villages near Dewsbury, West Yorkshire, 40
Hastings, battle of, 4
Hastings, Lady, Elizabeth, 83
Hawley, Thomas, 221
Haworth, 24, 25, 32, 47, 59, 62, 113, 171, 201, 208, 237, 243
Haymarket, London, 146
Heald, Rev., Tong Church, 124
Heap, Rev., Henry, 29, 34, 38, 91, 104, 123, 124, 156, 213, mention of portrait by Geller 241, mention of portrait by Branwell Brontë 243
Hearne, friend of Dr. Richardson, 3, 222
Heath Hall, near Wakefield, 179, 205
Heaton, Bradford, 5, 32, 44, early

school at 106, 201, home of "Blind Jimmy" 249
Heaton, William, poet, 239
"Heavy-coach", the, Bradford stage-coach, 153
Hebden Bridge, Calder valley, West Yorkshire, 64, 101
Heckmondwike, Kirklees, West Yorkshire, 12, 97, 99
Heineken, Rev., Nicholas T, Picture of 51, 51, 97, portrait by Geller 241
Hemingway, Henry, attorney, 205
Henry, Duke of Lancaster, 9, 24
Henry V, King, 24
Henry VI, King, 23
Henry VII, King, 109, 203
Henry VIII, King, 2, 13, 220
Henry, Farrar & Co., shop of, in Kirkgate 85
Hepworth, John, fortune-teller, 244
Heron J. N & Co., 155
Herschell, Sir, John, 91
Hetton, Johannes, Poll Tax list 11
Hey, Richard, On Duelling and Backing, 95
Heywood, Rev. Oliver, of Coley, 14, 25, friend of Jonas Waterhouse 31, 47, 48
Hick, Sammy, preacher, 249
Highbury, Training College, 37
"Highflyer", coach, 172, 177
Highflyer Row, Bradford Moor, 172
High Sheriff of Yorkshire, 220
High Street, 16, Sunday School in 103, 123, Duke of Wellington Inn 165
Highwaymen, 19
Hill, Charles, of the Golden Fleece Odd Fellows Lodge, 150
Hill, John, Maltster, 110
Hill, Jonas, landlord of the Nag's Head Inn, 175
Hill, Joseph, first manager of the Bradford Commercial Bank, 155, 161
Hill, Joseph, tea-dealer, 227
Hill, Mr., J. P, manager of the Bradford Commercial Bank, 161
Hill, Rowland, 156
Hinchcliffe, Joseph, Moravian, 74
Hinchcliffe, Joshua, Post office box-holder 156
Hird, Dawson & Hardy, firm of, 155
Hird, family, 218
Hird, Henry, 156, 189
Hird, James, writer & poet, *"A Voice from the Muse"* 239
Hird, (or Hurd), Sarah, wife of Joshua Bartlett, 210
Hird, Rev., Lamplugh, Prebendary of York, 111, 189, 201, 207
Hird, Richard, of Rawdon, 189
Hird, Sarah, Quaker, mother of Sarah Hird, 210
Hirst, Mr., Sun Hotel, 170
Hitchen, Hertfordshire, 214
Hoare, E, B, politician, 199
Hodgson, Captain, John, Cromwell's army, 14, 15
Hodgson, Mr., of Scolemoor, 69
Hodsden, Mrs., Dorothy, Claiming use of armorial bearings (1798) 201
Holcroft, Sir, Henry, 210
Holden, Angus, Preface xii, 172, picture of opposite 172, 199
Holden, Isaac, 86
Holder, Reuben, "popular rhymester", 247-248
Holdgate, Rev., Thomas, of Horton Lane Congregational Church, 70
Holdsworth, Dr., Vicar of Halifax, 220
Holdsworth, Jonathan, early member of Horton Lane Congregational Church, 70
Holgate, Mr., barber & toy seller, 228
Hollings & Sons, T., 155
Hollings, John, 43, 48, 89, 92, 155
Holloway, owner of a strolling theatrical company, 131, 132
Holme, the, the first Bradford factory,

illustration of, between pages 18-19
Holmes, Thomas, 155
Holroyd, Abraham, bookseller, poet, antiquary, 97, 161, 238, the *Bradfordian magazine* 238, his shop in Westgate 238, 239, picture of 239, his "*A Garland of Poetry by Yorkshire authors*" 239
Holyoake, orator, 151
Holy Trinity Church, Bradford, 44
Holy Trinity Church, Knaresborough, 29
Holywood House, County Down, 204
Hook, His *Roman History* 95
Hooley, (presumably a typo or alternative name for Howley near Batley), 48
Hope and Anchor Inn, Market Street, 118, 150, 171
Hope & Anchor Inn, Bank Street, 165, 171, illustration of 172, 227, 228
Hopper, Henry, "Hoppy", 80, 81
"Hoppy's bridge", 80
"Hoppy's House", 80
Horn, see Boar legend
Horn-blowing, tenure of, 9
Hornby Castle, Lune valley, Lancashire, 110, 174
Horneby, Willelmus de, 11, 12
Horse & Groom Inn, (later the Bee Hive Inn), 174
Horse Fair, 229
Horse Shoes Inn, Tyrrel Street, 165
Horsfall & Brothers, W., 156
Horsfall, J. G., 43, 91, 122, Returning officer 179
Horsfall's Mill, 58
Horsfall Turner, J., Preface xii, 50, 100, his "*Nonconformity in Idle*" 100
Horton, district of Bradford, 12, 13, 20, 27, 44, 49, Quaker burial ground 52, 54, 106, 113, 174, 201
Horton Baptist College, 66, 67, illustration of, facing page 101, 101-102, 155
Horton Delf, 48
Horton, Dionisia de, 12
Horton Grange, Legrams Lane, 213, 214
Horton Hall, 24, 31, 47, 48, 49, Wesley preached at 57, 101, 201, 209, 216, 217, illustration of 217, 218
Horton House, 101, 201
Horton House Academy, 74
Horton-in-Craven, North Yorkshire, 98
Horton Lane, 43, Ebenezer Chapel, 62, 68, 70, 76, 101, 104, 107, 149, 205, 243, 249
Horton Lane Congregational Church, 69, 70, Sunday School 70, 71, 104 illustration between pages 70-71, 73, new building, 73, 76, Sunday School 104, 107, 239, John Rushton sings at 247
Horton Lane Sunday School, 70-71
Horton Road, 20, 21, Wesleyan Octagon Chapel 59, 60, 62, 69, 76, 104, 171, 205, 207, 216
Horton, Tristram, priest in Bradford in The 16th century, 29
Hospital of St Peter's, York, 219
Houghton, Lord, 86, 87
Household suffrage, 180, 183
Howe, John, Puritan divine, 210
Howgill-Blackburn, publishers, 234
Howley Hall, near Batley, 48
Hoyland, Barbara, Quaker, 214
Hoylands, Quaker family, 54
Huckster's shop, Broadstones, 224
Huddersfield, West Yorkshire, 75, 137, 214, 233
Hudson, Edward, clerk (1840), 38
Hudson, John, postman, 154, illustration of 154
Hudson, Mr., Town Clerk, 190
Hudson, William, Post office box-

holder 155
Hull, East Riding of Yorkshire, 84, 138, 175, 177, 187, Hull Grammar School 187-188, 222
Hullcott, Buckinghamshire, 42
Hulme, Dr., physician, son of Samuel Hulme, 48
Hulme, Samuel, Presbyterian minister at Little Horton, 48
Hume, David, His *History of England* 95
Hunslet, Leeds, 247
Hunter, Thomas, tailor, 225
Hunt Yard, Great Horton, see Boar legend
Hustler & Blackburn, firm of, 155
Hustler & Seebohm, firm of, 155
Hustler, family, Quakers, of Bolton House, 54, 55, 56, 155, 212
Hustlergate, 116, 119, 161, 212
Hustler, John, 71, 91, 97, 103, 106, 212, 213
Hustler, John, Jnr., 103, 195, 212, 214
Hustler, John, Mentioned in the Quaker Registers (1745) 212
Hustler, Sarah, 214
Hustlers, Quaker family, 54, 56
Hustler, William, Mentioned in the Quaker Registers (1745) 212
Hutton, solicitor, in the firm of Killick, Hutton & Vint, 161

Ibbetson, James, printer, 235
Idle, village north-east of Bradford, 47, 51, 54, 99, 100, 208
Idle Independent Chapel, 51
Idle Moor, 51
Ilbert de Lacy, see Lacy
Illingworth, Alfred, manufacturer and MP, 191, 197, parliamentary election (1880) 198, election of (1885 and 1886) 199
Illingworth & Newboult, 226
Illingworth, Booth, builder and contractor, 127

Illingworth, J. A., 113
Illingworth, Jere, landlord of Bull's Head Inn, 165
Illingworth, John, draper, 226,
Illingworth, John, poet, 239
Illingworth, Miles, Post office box-Holder 155, *Bradford Observer* 236
Illingworth, Mrs., landlady, Bull's Head Inn, 169
Illiteracy, 105
Imperial Theatre, London, 144
Incorporated Church Building Society, 44
India, 188
Indulgence, Act of, (1672), 48
Industry, The, Lodge of the Independent Order of Odd-Fellows, 150
Infirmary, see Bradford Infirmary
Infirmary Street, 68, 74
Infirmary Street Chapel, 68, 74
Ingham, John, the constable, 111, 113
Ingham, Timothy, auctioneer & sheriff's officer, 228
Ingle, James, landlord of the Rawson's Arms Inn, 174
Ingle, William, son of James, 174
Inglis, Henry D, see "Derwent Conway"
Inkersley, Thomas, printer, publisher, book-seller and post-master, 41, 113, 119, 153, 154, his death 156, books printed by 234, 235
Inner Temple, the bar, London, 204
Inns & Hotels, of Bradford, 164-178
Inquisition (1277), 5
Inquisition (1311), 2, 6, 7, 8, 200
Inquisition (1361), 24
Inquisition, taken at Elland in Elizabeth's reign, 78
Inquisition, Charity Commissioners, 78
Institution for the Blind, 163
Irby, de, Rev., Richard, 38
Ireland, 46, 186, Forster's visit to

55

195, Forster appointed Chief Secretary of 198
"Iron-gates", dram shop, 174
Irving, Henry, actor, 149, 163
Isle of Wight, 42
Italy, 118
Ive-bridge, at the bottom of Ivegate, 20, 37
Ivegate, 8. 20, 37, 57, illustration of Toll Booth and old shops on, page opposite 109, Old Crown Inn 165, Unicorn Inn 166, 168, 170, 174, 195, 200, birthplace of John Sharp 217, 224, Hall of Pleas 226, picture of old Ivegate between 226-227, 227

Jackson, William, musical composer, 88, 163
Jacobitism, 74
Johnson, Benjamin, draper & hosier, 96
John Street, 110
James I, king, 200
James II, king, 31
James, John, author of History and Topography of Bradford, (1841), Preface xi, 2, 3, 4, 5, 6, 23, 28, 44, 45, 46, 48, 50, 51, 77, 79, 90, 91, 97, 119, 122, 156-157, 161, the "Continuation" of his "History of Bradford" 162, 171, Bradford elections 186, 189, 200, 205, 233, book published by Charles Stanfield 234, 238-239, 242, "History of Bradford" 243, 244
James Street (Westgate), 148
Jarratt, John, Claiming use of armorial bearings (1798) 201
Jefferson, Joseph, actor, 149
Jeffery, Herbert, solicitor, 161
Jennings, Mr., actor, 134
Jews, emancipation of the, 182
John, bishop of Lincoln, 38
Johnson, Ben, shopkeeper, 96, 225
John Street, 110

Joint Stock Bank, Halifax, 162
"Jolly Shoemakers" of Bradford, 174
Jones, Lloyd see Lloyd Jones
Jones, Maria, B, actress, 136, 142-143, picture of 142
Jones, Rev., J. Ceredig, 52
Jonson, Ben, 130
Jowett, Abraham, of Bowling, early Quaker, 52
Jowett, Nathan, 97
Judaism, 76
Judson, Thomas, early Quaker, 52
Jullien, Monsieur, 147
Just, Rev., E, 76

Kaye, Benjamin, Landlord of the Bee Hive Inn, 165, 174
Keeling, Rev., W, H, 81
Kean, Charles, Mr., & Mrs., actors, 126, 136, 147, 163
Keighley, Borough of Bradford, West Yorkshire, 92
Keighley, Edward, printer and bookseller, 225
Kell, S. C., 107
Kemble, actor, 126
Kemble, Mrs., Fanny, famous actress, 88
Kemp, Rev., Caleb, 29, 30, 38
Kempe, John, clerk (1639), 38
Kendal, Cumbria, 177
Kendal, Mrs., formerly Madge Robertson, actress, 148
Kendrew, Mr., shopkeeper, 227
Kenion, Edward, 190
Kennet, Rev., Benjamin, 38
Key, Thomas, Mr., of York, 102
Keys, Mr., druggist, 225
Kiel, W. C., Post office box-holder 155
Killick, Hutton, & Vint, solicitors, 161
King's Arms Inn, Westgate, 127, 165, 177
King's Head Inn, Westgate, 165,

189

Kipping, Thornton, 99
Kipping Chapel, Thornton, 69
Kirby, Joshua, of Wakefield, 47
Kirk, Miss, Lizzie, actress, 141
Kirk, Mrs., actress, sister of Mr., Mosley, 141
Kirkby Lonsdale, Cumbria, 158
Kirkgate, 3, 8, 20, 61, 79, 85, 91, 96, 103, 114, 136, 139, 140, post office on 152, 153, 154,, the "Old Bank" 158, Wentworth Bank 160, 162, Bishop Blaize Inn 165, Brown Cow Inn 165, Dog & Shovel Inn 165, Nag's Head Inn 165, Royal Oak Inn 165, Talbot Hotel 166, White Horse Inn 166, White Lion Inn 166, 168, 175, 179, 184, 200, 201, Manor Hall 203, 223, picture of Kirkgate in 1827 224, 224, picture of old shops on Kirkgate between 224-225, Allott's shop 225, John Nicholson printer 233, 235, the Brontë sisters seen in 237, 243, Thomas Ramsden's book-stall 248, 249
Kirkgate Chapel, Wesleyan Methodist, 61, 62, John Rushton sings at 247
Kirkgate Wesleyan Sunday School, 103
Kirkstall Abbey, 13 Christeal Abbey, 219
Kirkstall, Abbot of, 109
Kitchen, Thomas, early Quaker, 52
Knapton, Rev., J., 52
Knaresborough, North Yorkshire, 28, 29, 185, 203
Knight, J. W., artist, Preface xii
Knight, Titus, Wesleyan preacher, 65
Knowles, Sheridan, Irish dramatist and actor, 87, 130
Kossuth, Lajos, Hungarian political leader, 163

Lacy, Alice, de, wife of Thomas Earl of Lancaster, 24, 38
Lacy, de, family, 7, 9, 24, 77, 119
Lacy, Edmund de, 5, 119
Lacy, Henry de (Earl of Lincoln), 5, 6, 24, 200
Lacy, Ilbert de, baron of Pontefract, 4, 219
Lacy, John, of Cromwellbotham, married to Anne Tempest, 221
Laisterdyke, district of Bradford, 44, 80
Lamb, Mr., owner of private school, 84, 119
Lamb, Mrs., 119
Lambert, General, Civil War, 31
Lambert, Richard, 97
Lancashire & Yorkshire Railway Company, 55, 190
Lancashire & Yorkshire Railway Station, 213
Lancashire Cotton Famine, 146
Lancaster, Alice, 24
Lancaster, Blanche, daughter of Henry, Duke, 9
Lancaster Castle, 186
Lancaster, Earls of, 9
Lancaster, Henry Duke of, 9, 24
Lancaster, Lancashire, 9, 13, 24, 186, 218, 219
Lancaster, Maude of, daughter of Henry, Duke, 9
Langdale, Sir Marmaduke, 30
Lansdowne Place, Horton Lane, 76
Latrynton, de, Rev., Henry, (1335), 29, 38
Latter Day Saints, Church of, see Mormons
Law, Alderman, James, 70, 92
Laycock, Samuel, 43, 86, 88, 92, 160, *Bradford Observer* 236
Leach, Clayton & Co., 156
Leach, Rev., Henry, vicar of All Saints, 92, 93, 160
Leach, Pollard & Hardcastle, bank of, 19, 157

Leah, family, 218
Leah, Henry, 121, 231
Learoyds, Quaker family of Allerton, 54
Leaventhorp, William, fifteenth Century gentleman, 12, 28
"Lecturer", at the parish Church, 78, 80, 81
Lee, J. L., post office box-holder, 155
Lee, John, 113
Lee, William, custodian of the debtor's prison, 112
Leeds Intelligencer, newspaper, 236
Leeds, West Yorkshire, 13, 14, 16, 24, 57, 73, 75, 84, 92, 96, 153, 154, 157, 175, turn-pike mob at 176, 177, 178, 179, 180, W. E. Forster defeat as Liberal candidate at 195, 202, 209, 223, 233, Samuel Topham 242, 243
Leeds-Liverpool canal, 94, 203
Leeds-Liverpool Canal Co., 203
Leeds Mercury, newspaper, 236
Leeds Philosophical Society, 92
Leeds Road, 20, 54, 61-62. 85, 106, 150, Temperance Hall 213, old Leeds Road 223
Leicester, 24
Leicestershire, 221
Legard, Johannes, hosteller, Poll Tax list, 11
Legend of the boar, see Boar legend
Legrams Lane, 213
Leland, John, His *Itinerary* (c.1540), 2, 13, 14, 37
Leominster, Herefordshire, 204
Leventhorpe, William, 12
Leyden University, Holland, 222
Leyland, sculptor from Halifax, 171
Liberal Party, (Reform Party or Liberalism), 179, 182, 184, 186, 187, 188, 189, 190, W. E. Forster's support of 195
Liberal Registration Association, 197
Licensed Victuallers, 196
Licensing Justices, 165
Lidget Green, Bradford, 64
Light, (Haigh & Light), Post office box-holders, 155
Lincey, J. H., manager of Beckett & Co., Bank, 159
Lincoln, Preface xii, 5, 6, 24, 38, 200
Lincoln gaol, 30
Lincoln, Henry de Lacy, Earl of, 5, 6, 24, 200
Lincoln, John, bishop of, 38
Lincolnshire, 30, 221
Lind, Jenny, musician, 163
Lindley, Francis, son of William, 27, 222
Lindley, William, of Hull, father of Francis, 222
Linnell, artist, 242
Lister, Ellis Cunliffe, father of S. C. Lister, 20, 86, 111, 122, 155, 179, 180, picture of opposite page 180, 181, 182, 183, 184, 185, 198, 216, 250
Lister, G, T., Post office box-holder 156
Lister Hills, district west of Bradford town centre, 44, 73
Lister Hills Congregational Church, 73
Lister, John, of Manningham, "gentleman bearing arms" (1665), 201
Lister, Joseph, His "Genuine Account", 14, siege of Bradford 16, 82, 209
Lister, Mary, Claiming use of armorial bearings (1798) 201
Lister, Mr., of Shibden Hall, 79, 82
Lister Park, Manningham, 97
Lister, Richard, 38
Lister, Samuel **C**unliffe, son of E. C. Lister, Preface xii, 82, 180, 190, 216, picture of between pages 216-217

Lister statue, Preface xi
Lister, William Cunliffe, 185, 186, 198
Lister, William, landlord of the Angel Inn, 165
Literary Club, 108
Little Horton, 8, 48, 57, 64, 69, 73, Moravian society, 74, 101, 114, 216, Sharp family 217
Little Horton Congregational Church, 73
Little Horton Green, 103, 216
Little Horton Lane, 21, 205
Little Horton Moravian Chapel, 74
Liverpool, 35, 37, 67, 76, 144, 177, 241
Liverpool Institution, 37
Liversedge, Kirklees, West Yorkshire, 210
"Liver" Theatre, 135
Liveseys, Quaker family of Horton, 54
Livingstone, David, missionary and explorer, 163
Lloyd Jones, public orator, 151
Local government, 21, parish beadle 21, watchmen 21
Local preachers, 249
Lockwood & Mawson, Bradford architects, 161
Lockwood, H. F., architect, 192-193
London, 24, 30, 32, 51, 53, 68, 75, 84, 97, 99, 137, 139, 144, 146, 149, 152, 153, 154, 157, 175, 177, 189, College of Physicians 211, 212, 219, James Geller in 241, J. C. Bentley taught in,241, 242
London, SS, ship, sank (1866), 129
London, The, formerly the Bermondsey Hotel, 174
"Long Bottom's School", 127
Longfield, Mr., shopkeeper, 225
Long Pledged Teetotal Association, 107
"Looking Glass", series of tracts printed by Rev. William Atkinson against Dissent, 208
Loosemore, Rev., R. W., 43
Loraine, Mr., Henry, 140, 143
Lord Brougham, see Brougham, Lord
Lord Clifford, of Skipton Castle, 219
Lord Fairfax, see Fairfax, Thomas
Lord, Mr., of Bacup, Baptist, 62
Lord Nelson Inn, Northgate, 165
Lord of the Manor, 5, 8, 77, 104, 118, 124
Lord's Mill, 200
Loughnan, Rev., John E., 42
Lower Globe Fold, Manningham, 103
Low Fold, Bolton, Bradford, 195, 211
Low Moor, Bradford, 24, 50, 51, 56, 89, 136, 140, 185, 190, 202, 204, 218, 249
Low Moor Ironworks, John Hardy, partner in 179, 190, 218
Ludlow, Shropshire, 96
Lumb, George, Landlord of the Old Crown Inn, 165
Lumb, Joshua, Innkeeper, Old Bishop Blaize Inn, 165
Lumb Lane, 68, 208
Lund, Charles, tutor at the Mechanics Institute, 88
Lund, Mr., bookseller, 226
Lunefield, Kirkby Lonsdale. 158
Lupton & Son, R., 156
Lupton, John, landlord of the Bowling Green, 168
Lupton, Samuel, landlord of The Fleece Inn, 165
Lutheranism, 51
Luton, Bedfordshire, 215
Lyell, Prof., 91
Lymbergh, Adam de, presbyter, 38

Macauley, Mr., actor and elocutionist, 128, 130
Macclesfield, Cheshire, 51

Macdonald, George, Scottish author, poet and Congregational minister, 87
Mackay, Mr., actor, 137, 140, 141, 145
Macready, actor, 136, 139, 146, 147, 163
Macturk, Dr., 43, 91, 125, 133, his sister 206
Maddocks, priest at St Mary's Church, Stott Hill, 46
Magdalen Hall, Oxford, 37
Magistrates, 111, 113
"Mally", owner of huckster's shop, Broadstones, 224
Malmsbury, William of, 4
Malting, right of, 213
Malt Shovel Inn, 175
Manchester, 92, 96, 177, 182, 183, 189
Manchester Road, (formerly known as Bowling Lane), 42, 43, Primitive Methodist Chapel 62, 84, 101, "model school" in 106, 205
Mann & Co., J. T., firm of, 155
Manning, Cardinal, 163
Manningham, 11, 12, 13, 20, 43, 44, Quakers 52, 62, 73, 101, 103, early school at 106, 180, 201, 208, 249
Manningham, family of, 8
Manningham Hall, 111, 184, 216
Manningham Lane, Preface xii, 20, 40, 42, 68, 76, 78, 79, "Spotted House" 111, 142, site of new theatre 148, 215, 216, "Spotted House" 250
Mann, Joshua, 43, 121
Mann, Rev., Isaac, Baptist, 102
Mann, Thomas, 216
Mannville, Horton Road, 62
Mannville, House/villa, 216
Mannville, Methodist New Connexion Chapel and school, 62
Manor Court, 112, 164
Manor Court Rolls, Bradford, 5
Manor Hall, Hall or Aulum in Medieval period 6, 40, 118, 136, 152, 203-204, picture of the old doorway 204, illustration of Manor Hall in Kirkgate between pages 204-205, 205, 208, 229
Manor House, 175
Manorial Records, 8
Manor of Bradford, 4, 5, 6, 9
Manor of Bolling, see Bowling
Manor Row, 93
Manville School, Horton Road, 76
Manyngham, Margeria, 12
Margerison, Joseph, L., Preface xii, 89
Mariner's Church, Liverpool, 35
Market, Bradford, Earliest 5, 6, 7, 20, 103, 118-120, picture of the old Market House opposite 118, 121, Market Hall 152, 162, 169, 212, 228, 229, new Market Place 235, 249
Market Cross, 119, 120, picture of 120, 210
Market Hall, 104, 162, 205, 227, 228
Market House, 118-120, see also Market Hall and Market
Market Street, (formerly New Street), 20, 96, 103, 119, 121, 122, 127, theatre on 128, 151, 158, Bradford Banking Company 160, 161, Boar's Head Inn 165, Britannia Inn 165, Salutation Inn 165, Rawson's Arms 165, White Swan Inn 166, George Hotel 171, White swan Inn 172, 174, 194, 212, 223, 227, 228, 230
Market Tavern, 150, 175
Markham's *Life of the Great Lord Fairfax*, 15
Marmaduke, friend of Dr. Richardson, 222
Marsden, family, Lords of the Manor, 110
Marsden, Henry, of Gisburn, 110

Marsden, Henry of Wennington Hall, Lancashire, 110
Marsden, John of Hornby Castle, 110
Marshall, Grace, early Quaker, 52
Marshall, James, 231
Marshall, John, early Quaker, 52
Marston Moor, battle of, 47
Martin, Baron, 197
Martin, John, artist, 241, picture of the "Plains of Heaven" 241
Martin, Jonathan, 244
Martin, Mr., Post office box-holder 155
Martin, William, Chartist, Irish politician, 185, 186, 190
Mary Tudor, Queen, 45
Mary, wife of John Maynard of Tooting, 24
Mason, Miss, Librarian of the Subscription Library, 96
Mason, Nicholas, Landlord Nag's Head Inn, 165
Mason, Thomas, 222
Massachusetts, America, 190
Massinger, writer, 130
Masterman, William, 157-158
Maude, daughter of Henry, Duke of Lancaster, 9
Mauds, Quaker family, 54
Maud, William, surgeon, 113, 213, 214, 226
Maud & Wilson, firm of Chemists, Sunbridge, 213, 226
Mauritius, Islands in the Indian Ocean, 37, 38
Maw, Mr., W, Preface xii
Mawson, Nicholas, Landlord of The Nag's Head, 175
Maynard, Mary, wife of John Maynard of Tooting, 24, 38
Maynard, Sir John, 24, 31, 205
McArthur, local artist, Preface xi, xii, sketch of Union Passage 154
McCroben, John, early member of Horton Lane Congregational Church, 70, 189

McKay, William, early member of Horton Lane Congregational Church, 70
McKean, Tetley & Co's warehouse, 128
McTurk, Dr., see Macturk
Mead, Matthew, Puritan divine, 210
Mechanics' Institute, 51, 65, 72, 75, 83-88, sketch of the old Mechanic's Institute, Leeds Road 85, 86, opening of the new building 1871, 87, public lectures 87, 88, 93, 151, 162, 163, supported by John Hardy 179, 230, Geller's portrait of Steadman at 241
Melbourne, Australia, 36
Menai Straits, North Wales/Anglesey, 207
Mercer, Mrs., Librarian of the Subscription Library, 96
Methodism, see Wesleyan Methodism, Methodist New Connexion, Primitive Methodism, Free Methodism and Wesleyan Reformers
Methodist New Connection, 62, Ebenezer Chapel 62, Chapel in Horton Road 62
Miall, Edward, 194, 196-197, 198
Miall, L. C., 93
Miall, Rev., James G., Congregationalist minister and historian, 73, 88, 92, *"History of Congregationalism in Yorkshire"* 239, *"Memorials of Early Christianity"* 239, *"Footsteps of our Forefathers"* 239, *"Yorkshire Illustrations"* 239, Salem Congregational Church 239
Michaelis & Samson, firm of, 155
Microscopical Society, 108
Middleton, Sir Hugh, 24
Midgley, Martha, Landlady, Roebuck Inn, 165
Midgley, Mary, Church-cleaner, 741
Midland Railway, 177, 178

Midland Station, 224
Mildred, Masterman & Walker, bankers, London, 157
Militia, see Volunteer Corps
Mill, water & fulling, 2, 6
Mill Bank, 8, 103
Miller, David Prince, strolling player, 132
Millergate, 152, 231
Milligan & Son, J., 155
Milligan, Forbes & Co., 153, 155, 189
Milligan, Robert, 70, 86, 153, 188-189, appointed Mayor and MP 189, 190, 191, 198, 236
Mill Goit, "Mill-race", Silsbridge Lane, 65, 66
"Milling & Malting", right of, 213
Milner, Johannes, Poll Tax list 11
Milnes & France, architects, 161
Milnes & Wilcock, 156
Milnes, William, early member of Horton Lane Congregational Church, 70
Milthorp, John, Post office box-holder 156
Milthorp, Thomas, 113, 155
Milthorpe & Co., Thomas, 155
Mirfield, William de, 38
Miryshaw, mansion in Barker-end, 201, 205
Mitchell, E. J., 89
Mitchell, Mr., Post office box-holder 156
Mitchell, Thomas, Methodist lay preacher, 57-58
Mitton, Rev., Canon, 43
Monastic fairs, 7
Montgomery, James, 92
Moore, Sir John, 231
Moravians, (United Brethren), 73-74, at Leeds, Wakefield, Bingley and Halifax 73, Fulneck 73, Little Horton 74, Paternoster Fold 74, 75
More, William, suff., Bishop of Colchester, 38

Morgan, Rev., William, of Christ Church, 39, 40, 41, his "Life of Rev John Crosse" and other writings 42, 71, 213, his support of his relative Branwell Brontë 243
Morgan's News Room, 175
Morgan, William, caterer and theatre manager, 39, 40, 148, 149
Morley, near Leeds, 12, 215, 225
Mormons, (Latter Day Saints), 151
Morpeth, Lord Viscount, MP, 86, 118
Morrie, Francis, 38
Mortimer, James, see "Blind Jimmy"
Mortlake, in Surrey, 209
Moryn, Robert, Chaplain, (1327), 38
Mosley, John, actor and proprietor of a theatre company, 129, 135, 136, 137, Mosley and Rice theatrical company 139-142, 141, 142, 143, 144, 145, 146, 147
Mossman, G. R., (also spelled as Mossmann), 89, 97, 125, 156
Moulden, William, Post office box-holder 155
Muff, Mr., milliner, brother-in-law of Henry Brown, 226, 228, picture of Brown & Muffs old shop 228
Mumford & Johnson, solicitors, 161
Murchison, Roderick, 91
Murgatroyd, William, 86, 156
Murgatroyd & Clayton, firm of, 155
Murphy, Rev., Francis, 45-46, pamphlet war with Rev J. Taylor, curate of the parish Church

Nag's Head Inn, Kirkgate, 115, 139, 165, 175
Nantwich, battle of, 47
Napoleonic Wars, 83
Nash, Rev., A. J. G., 43
Naturalist's Society, 108
Neesom, brothers, grocers & hop merchants, 227
Nelson, Arthur, clown & strolling player, 132
Nelson, John, stonemason,

62

Methodist Preacher, Picture of Nelson in Bradford gaol, between pages 57-58, imprisoned in a dungeon in Ivegate 57, 94, 111, 249
Neptune Inn, the, 27
Nesbit, Anthony, 127
Newall Hall, (Otley, West Yorkshire), 176
Newark College, Leicester, (College of the Blessed Mary), 24
Newboult, George, Preface xii, 88
New-bridge, 20
Newcastle, Earl of, (Royalist), See Civil War, 16, 17, 209, 221
New Church, see Swedenborgianism
New College, Oxford, 189
New Inn, the, 91, 110, Tyrrel Street, 165, 169
New Leeds School, 106
New Market Street, 230 see also under Market Street
Newspapers, 235-236, see entries for *Bradford Courier, West Riding Advertiser, Bradford Daily Telegraph, Bradford Observer,* Bradford Times, the *Bradford & Wakefield Chronicle, Leeds Mercury* and the *Leeds Intelligencer*
New Street, (later Market Street), 119
Newton, Rev., Robert, Methodist, 249
New York, America, 209
Nichelson, Adam, Medieval Poll Tax list 11
Nichol, James, publisher, 210
Nicholson, George, son of John Nicholson, printer, 96, 233
Nicholson, John, organ builder, 89
Nicholson, John, printer, 95, 96, 233, 246
Nicholson, John, the "Airedale-poet", 127, the play "Robber of the Alps" 127, "The Siege of Bradford" 127, 128, 233-234, Charles Stanfield publishes his poems 234, 235, 237-238, picture of his birthplace 238, portrait of by Geller 241, 246, his criticism of Reubon Holder 247
Nicholson, Mary, 96
Nicholson, R., Post office box-holder, 155
Nicholson, Samuel, son of John Nicholson, printer, 96, 233
Nicholson, Thomas, poet, brother of John Nicholson, 239
Nidd Hall, near Knaresborough, 203
Norfolk, county of, 206, 207
Norfolk, Duke of, 221
Norman Conquest, 1
Northallerton, North Yorkshire, 10, 186
Northallerton gaol, 186
Northallerton House of Correction, 186
North, Arthur, artist, Preface xii,
North Bierley, 12, 113, 201
Northern Baptist Education Society, 101
Northern Education Society, 97
"Northern Worthies", book by Hartley Coleridge, 171
Northgate (formerly Fair-gap or "Fayre Gappe"), 20, 40, Lord Nelson Inn, 165, 208
North, John, poet, 239
Northorp, Johannes de, 12
Northowram, near Halifax, 99
Northowram Academy, 99
North Parade, 215
North, Quaker family, 54
Northrop, John, of Manningham, 9
Northrop, William, parish clerk, 29
Northrops, family of, 8
Northumberland, 4
North Wing, Bradford, 112
Norton, William de, presbyter, 38
Norwich, Norfolk, 210
Norwood, C. M., politician, 199
Nottingham, 99
Nunn, John, of the Theatre Royal,

174
Nunn, Miss, Annette, actress, 138
Nunn, Mr., "Jack", 138, picture of 138, proprietor of the Bermondsey Hotel 138
Nunn, Mr., lace-maker, "Jack" Nunn's Uncle, 138
Nunn, Mrs., actress, 137, 138, Landlady of the Bermondsey Hotel 138, 142, 143,144
Nunnely, T, Mr., 92
Nutbrowne, William, ale-taster, 164

Oastler, Richard, 42, 218, statue of 218
Oastler's Monument, 174, 218
Oates, Henry, 97
Oates, Henry William, 231
Observer Office, 236
Octagon Chapel, Wesleyan Methodist, Horton Road, 21, 59, 60, illustration of 60, 61, Sunday School 104
Odd-fellows, Independent Order of, 129, 130, 150
Odd-fellows' Arms, Manchester Road, 84
Odd-fellows' Hall, Thornton Road, 129, 130, 150-151, illustration of 150, 163
Odd-fellow's Hall Theatre, 131
Oddy, Mark, rope maker, 227
Odsal House, 218
Okden, Thomas, clerk (1556), 38, 79
Okell, John, 38
Old Back Lane, 165
Old Bell Chapel, Horton, 44, 174
Old Bishop Blaize Inn, Westgate, 165
Old Bradford Bank, See Bradford Bank, 157, illustration of 157, 158
Old Bradford families, 200-222
Old Brewery, Horton Road, 69, 73, 207
Old Brewery, Thornton Road, 230, 231

Old Butter Market, Preface xi
Old Church steps, 166
Old Court House, 226, see also Court House
Old Crown Inn, Ivegate, 165, 169
"Old Enquirer", pen-name used by the Rev. William Atkinson, 208
Oldfield, William, Bee Hive Inn, 174
Old foundry, 207, 230, picture of 230
Old Hall, Stott Hill, 157
Old Justice Court, 110, picture of 110
"Old Justice Room", 110
Old Leeds Road, 223
Old Manor House, Morley, 215
Old Market, 103, 169
Old Market Hall, 104, 228
Old Market House, Preface xi
Old Soke Mill, see Soke Mill
Old Stream, or Goit, 231
Old Unitarian Chapel, Illustration of in between pages 47-48, 49
Old vicarage, see Vicarage
"Old Wild", Jemmy Wild, 132
"Old Wild's", travelling theatre group, 128
Olney, Buckinghamshire, 102
"Operative Conservative Association", 185
"Orange & Protestant Minstrel" (1852), by Squire Auty, 235
Order of the Holy Trinity, Knaresborough, 29
Oriel College, Oxford, 204
Orr, James, of Holywood House, County Down, 204
Orr, Jane, wife of Lord Cranbrook, 204, 205
Osborne & Co., G, 156
Osborne House, 146
Otley, West Yorkshire, 49, 233
Otley Road, 44
Otway, writer, 130
Oundle, Northamptonshire, 137
Ourom, Ricardus de, 11
Ouroune, Henricus de, 11

Outhwaite, Dr., 97, 121, 125, post office box-holder 155
Outhwaite, Mr., chemist, 225
Outhwaite, Thomas, 97
Owen, John, Dr., 209
Owen, Robert, manufacturer, philanthropist and social reformer, 151
Oxford, 30, 37, 67, 189, 190, 204, 222
Oxford Baptist Church, 67
Oxford University, 190, 222

Pack horses, 175
Pack Horse Inn, Westgate, 165, 225
Paley, family, 218
Paley, John Green, of the Bowling Iron Works, 160, 222
Paley, Mr., 222
Palmerston, Lord, 122, 163, 190, 191,
Pamphlet, "the errors, corruptions, and Claims of the Church of Rome ....", 45-46
Pantomimes, 142, 149
Paper Hall, Barkerend, 69, illustration of the back of 108, full description of 202, picture of the Old Paper Hall 202, ghost story relating to 203, see reference to James Garnett.
Parish beadle, 21
Parish Church see Church, parish
Parish Church Registers, 14, 164
Parkinson, Robert, chemist, 229
Parkinson, seller of tobacco & snuff, 228
Park Road, 102
Parliament, 180, reformed parliament (1832) 181, 182, 186, 189, 191, 194, W. E. Forster at 195, 197, 204
Parliamentary elections, 111, 168, 179-199 and see Elections
Parliamentary Survey of Church Livings (1650), 27

Parochial schools, 36, 89, 106, Parochial School Fund 106,
Parrish's, strolling theatre company, 131
Pateley Bridge, North Yorkshire, 161
Paternoster Fold, Great Horton, 74
Patterson, R., 155
Paull, village in the East Riding, 189
Pawson, Samuel, landlord, Pack Horse Inn, 165
Pearson, Andrew, Quaker, 56
Pearson & Son, William, 155
Pearson, John, 121
Pearson, Quaker family, 54
Pearson, Rev., C. J., 43
Pearson, Robert, early Quaker, 52
Peckover & Ferrand, firm of, 155
Peckover, Edmund, 97, 119, 157, 158, 202
Peckover, family, Quakers, 54
Peckover House, 62
Peckover, Joseph, 103, 158
Peckover Park, 106, 158
Peckover Street, 123
Peel Park, 72, 120, 168
Peel, Sir, Robert, 168
Peel Square, 128
Peel's Statue, 150, 168
Peile, Benjamin, dyer, 231
Pemberton, Rev., Francis, 25, 27, 38
Pendle Hill, Lancashire, 101
Penny-Post, the, 156
Penny, the tailor, 226
Penzance, Cornwall, 40, 41
"People's Charter" (Chartism), 186, 188
Perkyn, Elizabeth, Poll Tax list 12
Phelps, actor, 136, 147
Philharmonic Society, 118, 169
Phillip, Francis, Church patron, 38
Phillips, Mr., 141
Phillips, Mr., junior, 141
Phillips, Prof., 91
Philosophical Society, 36, 90-93, 108, 212

Piccadilly, 85, 96, 120, 122, 152, 155, 156, 236
Pickard, "brother", preacher, 250
Pickering, North Yorkshire, 34
Pickersgill, H. W., artist, Page facing 179
Piece Hall (1773), 19, 91, 110, 114-118, illustration of 114, 118, 121, 179
Pilcher, Rev., Richard, 52
"Pilgrimage of Grace", (1536), 220
Pillory, bottom of Westgate, 168
Piper's Grave, 40
Pitt, Charles, actor, 147
Pitt, William, politician, 180
Plague, the, see Black Death
Plantagenet, Kings, 1, 10-11
"Pleasure fair", 229-230
Plumbe, John, of Tong, 221
Plumbe, Miss, 221
Plumbe, Richard, 99
Plymouth, Devon, 52
Police, the, 197
Polish Historical Society, 92
Pollard & Co., 155
Pollard, family, 8, 83, 218
Pollard, George, 91
Pollard, Joseph, Landlord of the Boar's Head Inn, 165, 174
Pollard, Joshua, 218
Poll Tax, for Manningham (1378), 5
Poll Tax, of Richard II, 11, 12
Pontefract, West Yorkshire, 4, 6, 12, 30, 111, 180, 233
Pontefract Castle, 4, 30, 221
Poor Law Bill, 36
Poor Law Board, 204
Poor Law Riots (1837), 114, 185
Pope, Alexander, His trans. of Shakespeare 95
Popplewell, B. B, Mr., spirit merchant, 174
Population, of Bradford, Medieval 6-7, 13, Irish 46, (population in 1801) 19-20, 21
Postmaster General, 152, 153, 154
Post Office, 119, 122, 151-156, illustration of the old Post Office in Millergate 152, 162, 167
Post Office Savings' Bank, 162
Post Office Yard, see Union Passage
Pottenger, Rev., Thomas, Baptist, 68
Potter, Thomas, 88, 107
Poughil, near Ludlow, Shropshire. 96
Powell, Francis Sharp, 216, 217
Presbyterian Church, Chapel Lane, 69
Presbyterianism, 48, 69, Infirmary Street Chapel, 74
Preston, Ben, poet and writer, 161, 238-239
Preston, Isabella de, Medieval Poll Tax list 12
Preston, Miss, Mary, Claiming use of armorial bearings (1798) 201
Preston, William de, Chaplain, 38
Price, Morton, Mr., 147
Priestley, Captain, John, 203
Priestley, Dr., Joseph, scientist & philosopher, 50, 90, 95, 97
Priestley, Joseph, 50, 203
Priestley, Mr., actor, 134
Priestley, Mr., of Stott Hill House, 94
Priestley Street, 203
Priestley, Timothy, 99
Priestman, John, 92, 194, 213, 231
Primitive Methodism, 62
Prince of Wales, 90, visit to Bradford (1882) 223
Prince Rupert, Civil War, 30
Prince's Theatre, Horton Lane, 43, 149
Prison, "old lockup", Sunbridge, 111, beneath the Toll-Booth 111, "Nelson's dungeon" 57, 111, a room in the Cock-pit 111, "Will Lee Hoil", the debtors prison 112
Pudsey, near Leeds, West Yorkshire, 47, Quakers at 52, 113, 208
Pullan, J., Post office box-holder 155

Pullan, Messrs, 149
Pullan, Thomas, 231
Punishment, Medieval methods of, 109
Puritanism, 14, 18, Caleb Kemp 29-30, 47, 52, 120, 126, Robert Clarkson 208, Dr. John Owen 209, 210, Baxter, Howe and Mead 210
Pyrmont, Germany, 214

Quack-doctors, 229
Quaker Biblical names, 53
Quaker burial ground, Horton, 52
Quakerism (Society of Friends), John Wynn 19, 21, 52-56, occupations of early Quakers 54, old Quaker family names 54, teaching mentioned and praised 56, Quaker dress 56, Quaker School 106, 159, the Forster family 195, Sarah Hird 210, Benjamin Bartlett 211, John Fothergill 211, Ackworth School 211, Philanthropy 212, William Maud 213, Seebohm's upbringing 214, Stephen Grellet, Quaker preacher 214, Brighouse Monthly Meeting 214, Barbara Hoyland, preacher 214
Quaker Lane, Horton, 52
Quaker Register, Bradford, 210
Quaker Register of Births (1652), 52
Quaker Register of Burials, 52
Quaker School, 106
Quaker School, Chapel Street, 106, 212
Quaker School, Tottenham, 195
"Quaker Wilson", See William Wilson
Quarter Sessions, 190
Queensbury, 116, 224
Queen's flour Mills, (also called old Soke Mills), 231
Querical Society, 170

Radicals, 182, 185, 196
Raikes, Robert, of Gloucester, 103
Railway Bill, 177
Railways, Leeds to Selby line 84, 177-178, Midland Railway 177, 178, Lancashire & Yorkshire Railway Company 190
Ramsbotham, Robert, 97, 206
Ramsden, David, 190
Ramsden, Henry & Co., 155
Ramsden, John, of Haworth, "Gentleman bearing arms" (1665) 201
Ramsden, Sir John, 30
Ramsden, "Tommy" Thomas, auctioneer, book-seller in Kirkgate 248, picture of 248
Rand & Sons, 155, 190
Rand, family, 206
Rand, John, Jnr., 206, philanthropy 206, Churchman 206, picture of 206
Rand, John, Senior, 71, 91, 92, 97, 121, 155, 190, 206, 213
Rand, William, 86, 89, 206-207
Randal Well, Bradford, 216
Raper, John, Landlord of the King's Arms, 165
Rawdon, near Leeds, West Yorkshire, 52, 67, Baptist College 101, 102, 189, residence of W. E. Forster 195
Rawson & Co., 155
Rawson, Benjamin, Lord of the Manor, 40, 104, 110, 118, 124, purchases Nidd Hall 203
Rawson, Clayton & Co., 155
Rawson, Elizabeth, 112, 203
Rawson family, 203
Rawson, George & Wade, solicitors, 161
Rawson, John (1530), 29, 109
Rawson, John, solicitor, 29, *Bradford Observer* 236
Rawson, Mary, 112

Rawson, Mr., Lord of the Manor, 118
Rawson, Mrs., Frances, Claiming use of armorial bearings (1798) 201
Rawson Place, 128
Rawson's Arms, Market Street, 161, 165, 174
Rawson, William, 152, 203
Rawson, William, of Shipley, "gentleman bearing arms" (1665), 201
Rawsthorne, Walker, architect, 42
Ray, friend of Dr. Richardson, 222
Rayment, Rev., Benedict, of York, 45
Read, Benjamin, tinner & brazier, 227
"Ready-and-Steady", name given to Volunteer Corp (1794), 19
Reany, Miss, George Hotel, 171
"Rebecca" rioters, 176
Record Office, London, 219
Rector, Robert, 38
Rectory of St Nicholas, Guildford, 37
Re-distribution of Seats' Act, 198
Reed, Mr., H. B., 199
Reeves, Sims, "the great tenor", 147
Reformation, the, 1, 28, 44
Reform Bill, 118, 179, 180, 181, 191, 193, 250
Regiment, 32nd., of foot, 119
Reid, Dr., His *Inquiry into the human Mind* 95
Reid, Mr., T., Wemyss, Author of "*Life of the Right Honourable W. E. Forster*", 198
Reid, Wagstaff, J., solicitor, 85, 113
Rendell, J. Robson, Swedenborgian, "New Church" pastor, 75
Rennie & Tetley, firm of, 155
Repeal of the Game Laws, 183
Resolution, the, Ship on which William Scoresby and his father served 35
Restoration, the, of the Monarchy (1660), 18, 31, 47, 78
Reynolds, Sir Joshua, artist, 241
Rhodes, Charles, printer, 114, 125, 226
Rhodes, Manoah, watchmaker and silversmith, 225, picture of Rhode's shop 225
Rhodes, Miss, librarian, 96
Rhodes, Timothy, landlord, Ship Inn, 165
Ricardi, Margareta, Medieval Poll Tax List 12
Ricardi, Robertus, son of, Medieval Poll Tax list 11
Ricardi, Willelmus, son of, Medieval Poll Tax list 12
Rice, Charles, 135, 136, 137, Mosley and Rice theatrical company 139-140, 141, 143, 149, picture of appearing as "Rip Van Winkle" 149
Rice, Mrs., wife of Charles, dress designer for the theatre, 149
Rich, Mr., tea dealer, 226
Richard II, King, 7, 9, 11
Richards, Rev., John, 81
Richardson, Dr., of Bierley Hall, 3, 82, 212, 222, portrait of by Geller 241
Richardson, Mr., of Southowram, 93, 130
Richardson, T, M, artist, 240
Richardson, William, of North Bierley, "gentleman bearing arms" (1665), 201
Richmond, Rev., Legh, Author of the "*Dairyman's Daughter*", his visit to Bradford (1814) and his description of John Crosse 33
Richmond, Surrey, 205
Ricketts, Sir, Cornwallis, of Leicestershire, 221
"Riding of the boundary", manorial custom, 112
Ridehalgh, Richard, solicitor, 89, 161
Right of Gallows, 5

Rio de Janeiro, Brazil, 137
Ripley & Son, Edward, 156
Ripley's Dyeworks, Picture of between pages 196-197
Ripley, Sir, Henry, W., 70, 83, 86, 92, 93, created a baronet 197, 198
Ripon Church Building Society, 44
Ripon, North Yorkshire, 43
Risden, James, Landlord of the Boar's Head Inn, 174
Rishworth, Thomas, 121
Roads, 20, miserable condition of 175-176, see entry for Turn-pikes
Roberti, Alicia, Medieval Poll Tax list 12
Roberti, Christiana, Medieval Poll Tax list 12
Roberti, Johannes, Medieval Poll Tax list 12
Robertshaw, Benjamin, Landlord, Sun Inn, 165
Robertson, Madge, Miss (later Mrs., Kendal), actress, 148, 149
Robertson, William, *History of Scotland*, 95
Robinson, Mr., scene-painter and actor, 137, 141
Robson, Isaac, of Huddersfield, 214
Rochdale, a town in Lancashire, today Greater Manchester, 177
Rocket, Dudley, bookseller & businessman, 94
"Rockingham Bob", coach and four, 175
Rodes, Eliste, 29
Rodes, Matilda, 29
Rodes, William, presbyter, 29, 38
Roebuck Inn, Sunbridge, 45, 165, 175
Roebuck passage, in Market Street, 121
Rogers, G, (Leeds & West Riding Bank), post office box-holder 156
Rogers, Mr., actor, 129, 136
Rogers, Mr., G., 86, 156

Rogerson, Mr., shopkeeper, 161
Roman Catholic Chapel, Bradford, 124
Roman Catholicism, 44-46, 79, Bradford Roman Catholic Chapel 124
Romans, the ancient, 1, 3
Rookes, John, of Royds Hall, 27
Rookes, William, of Royds Hall, 202
Rose Cottage, at Low Fold, Bolton, Bradford, Residence of W. E. Forster 195
Ross, A. G., Post office box-holder 155
Rosse, Earl of, 93
Rossendale, Lancashire, 246
Rotherham, South Yorkshire, 99
"Rothsay Castle", wrecked ship (1831), 207
Roughton, Mr., 137, 141
Rouse & Sons, 155
Rowe, writer, 130
Royal Alexandra Theatre, Manningham Lane, 148
"Royal Mail", stage-coach, 153, 177
Royal Oak Inn, Kirkgate, 165
Royal Theatre, see Theatre Royal
Royalty Theatre, East End, London 137
Royds Hall, 27, 50, 91, 201, 202, 218
Rubenstein, musician, 163
Rubini, famous tenor, 147
Rugby School, Rugby, Warwickshire, 195
Rules and Regulations for woollen manufacturers, 116
Rupert, Prince, Siege of Pontefract Castle, Civil War 30
Rush, notorious murderer, (1849), 135
Rushton, John, poet, opponent of Southcottians, 246-247
Rushton, Mary Ann, daughter of John Rushton, 247
Rushton, Sarah, daughter of John,

247

Rushworth, of Horton, 9, 10
Ruskin, John, art critic and reformer, 27, 87
Russell, John, early member of Horton Lane Congregational Church, 70
Russell, John, Post office box-Holder 155
Russell, Lord, John, 179
Russell, Peter, shopkeeper, 225
Ryan, Rev., Vincent John, vicar of Christ Church, 42
Ryan, Right Rev., Dr., Vincent William, bishop of the Mauritius, 37, 38
Ryland, Rev., J, H., 51, 88

Sachs, Albert, photographer, Preface xii, credit on photograph opposite 216 and opposite 172
Sackville Street, 127
Saffery, J. Baptist preacher, 66
St Andrew, feast of, 6
St Andrew's Church, Lister hills, 44
St Ann's Church, Guy Street, (Roman Catholic), 46
St Augustine, 88
St Augustine's Church, Otley Road, 44
St Barnabas' Church, Heaton, 44
St Bartholomew, 81
St Bartholomew's Church, 44
St. George, Miss, Julia, actress, 136, 137, 139
St George's Hall, 68, C. H. Spurgeon preached there 68, 82, 89, 90, 107, 151, 163, Dickens reads from "Christmas Carol" at 171, speech by John Bright 191, 192
St Gregory, 28
St Ives, near Bingley, 203
St James' Church, Manchester Road, 42
St John the Evangelist Church, Great Horton, 44
St Johns' Church, Bowling, 43
St Johns' Church, Manchester Road, 42-43
St Joseph's Church, Packington Street, (Roman Catholic), 46
St Jude's Church, Bowling, 43, 89
St Luke's Church, 44
St Luke's Church, Manningham, 44
St Mark's Church, Manningham, 44
St Martin, feast of, 6, 8
St Mary's Abbey, York, 92
St Mary's Chapel, Stott Hill, (Roman Catholic), 45, illustration of, 45, 46, new Chapel on East Parade 46
St Mary's Church, Laisterdyke, 44
St Mary Magdalene's Church, White Abbey, 44
St Matthew's Church, Bankfoot, 43
St Michael and All Angels Church, 44
St Nicholas, 37
St Patrick's Church, (Roman Catholic), Westgate, 46
St Paul's Church, Manningham, 43, 249
St Peter's Church, Allerton, 44
St Peter's Church, Bradford see Church, Parish
St Peter's Church, Leeds Road, (Roman Catholic), 46
St Peters Church, York, 29
St Philip's Church, Girlington, 44
St Sitha, see Chapel of St Sitha
St Stephen's Church, 44
St Thomas' Church, 44
Salem Congregational Chapel, Manor Row, 73, Rev., J. G. Miall 239
Salt, Daniel, 156, 215
Salt, Daniel & Son, firm of, 215
Salt, Sir, Titus, 70, 82, 86, 155, 190, 191, 192-194, picture of 192, retires from Parliament 194, becomes baronet 194, parliamentary election (1859) 198,

early residence 207, Salt's Statue 207, 215, Old Manor House, Morley, Salt's birthplace 215, picture of the old Manor House 215, his philanthropy 215, use of alpaca 216

Saltaire, Titus Salt's model village near Bradford, 192, 239

Salutation Inn, Market Street, (also known as the Soldier & Sailor), 165, 174

Saracen's Head, Inn, Westgate, 165

"Saul", eccentric Methodist local preacher, 249

Savile, Henry, of Thornhill Green, "gentleman bearing arms" (1665), 201, 222

Savile, Sir William, Royalist commander, 16

Savings' Bank, 213

Saxons, the, 1, 3-4, 5

Sayers, Mr., post-master, 156

Scarborough, North Yorkshire, 10

Scarr Hill, Bradford Moor, 218

Scerlonis, Agnus, daughter of, Medieval Poll Tax list 12

Scharpe, Alicia, Medieval Poll Tax list 12

Schlesinger, Mr., Post office box-holder 155

Schofield, John, Preface xii

School Board, Bradford, 72

Schools, See Education, Parochial schools, Bradford Grammar School, "Model School" Manchester Road 106, "New Leeds School" 106, the "Daisy Hill School" 106, school at Eccleshill 106, see Quakerism, Stott Hill School 106, Schools at Heaton, Manningham, Bowling, Sticker Lane and Croft Street 106, see Female Educational Institute, Borough West Schools

School Street, 104

Scholemoor, Bradford, 69

Scholes, Dom William, 29

Schuster, Leo, of Manchester, 156, 189

Scientific Association, 108

Scoresby, Rev., Dr., William, 26, 34, arctic explorer and whaler 35, studied at Cambridge, curate of Bessingby, 35, Mariners Church, Liverpool, 35, his book "The Arctic Regions" 35, disputes over Church rates 35, his work to reduce hours for children in factories, 35, parochial schools 36, 106, Bradford Philosophical Society 36, Church Institute 36, trip to Australia 36, 38, dispute with Rev. C. J. Pearson 43, 88, founding of Church Institution 88, 89, philosophical society 91, titles of lectures given at 91, 106, 167, prolific writer 239

Scoresby, William, father of Dr. Scoresby, 34

Scottish raids, 10

Scott, Abraham, Church clerk (1832), 41

Scott, James, 97, 98, 99

Scott, John, animal engraver, 242

Scott, Mr., Scott's Academy, 97

Scott, Mrs., Landlady of the Bermondsey Hotel, 174

Scott, Rev., Walter, Congregationalist, 73, 88, 101

"Scratcher", seller of stone, 48

Scruton, William, author of the book, Preface, xi, xii

Sebastopol, Crimea, 146

Sedbergh School, Cumbria, 211

Sedgwick, Amy, actress, 136, 144, 145, 146

Sedgwick, Matthew, 97

Sedgwick, Prof., 91

Sedgwick, Richard, printer & bookseller, 226, 233

Seebohm, Benjamin, 71, 85, 213, 214, picture of between pages 214-215, "Memoirs of William Forster" by Seebohm 214

Seebohm, Frederick, 215
Seebohm, Henry, 215
Seebohm, Ludwig, father of Benjamin, 214, 215
Seebohm, "Private Memoirs of E. & B. Seebohm", 55, 214
Siege of Bradford see Civil War
Selby, North Yorkshire, 12, 15, 84
Selby, Samuel, Post office box-Holder 155
Selwyn, W. M., 89
Semon, Charles, 92
Separation of Church and State, see Disestablishment
Settle, North Yorkshire, 157
Sewell, watchmaker, 226
Shakespeare, William, 95, 125, 129, 130, 134, 138, 139, 140, 147
Shalders, Josephine, actress, 144
Shalloons, pieces of cloth, 114
Sharp, Abraham, mathematician of Horton Hall, 24, 47, 49, 82, 217
Sharp, Archbishop of York, 217
Sharp, Dr., 121, 125
Sharp, Elizabeth, daughter of Rev Thomas Sharp, 49
Sharp, family, 31, 217
Sharp, Isaac, 217
Sharp, John, of Horton Hall, 24, 47, 82, 208, 209, 217
Sharp, John, of Horton old Hall, Royalist, second cousin of John of Horton Hall, 217
Sharp, Rev., Thomas, of Horton Hall, and Adel, 47, 48, 49, 82, 208, 209, 217
Sharp, Samuel, of Leeds, 92
Sharp, Thomas, divine, 82, 208
Sharp, William, surgeon, 91, 92, 121, 125
Sharpe, C. S. B., Claiming use of armorial bearings (1798), 201
Shaw-Lefevre, G. J., politician, 199
Sheffield, South Yorkshire, 12, 61, 100, 137, 183, 233
Shepherd, Alexander, artist, Preface xii

Sheriff's Turn Court Leet, 8
Sherwood, Rev., W, 42, 89
Shibden Hall, near Halifax, West Yorkshire, 79, 82
Shields, Thomas, founder & proprietor of the *Bradford Daily Telegraph*, 237
Shiloh, promise of, 246
Ship Inn, Well Street, 165, 174
Shipley, Bradford, 12, 27, 32, Quakers at 52, 201, 221
Shipton, Old Mother, 244
Shirley, Miss, Beatrice, actress, 148
Shore, J, E, actor, 129, 136
Shoulder of Mutton, Inn, Kirkgate, 115, 165, 175
Shrewsbury School, Shropshire, 204
Sieges of Bradford, Civil War period, 14-18
Sierra Leone, West Africa, 188
Silsbridge Lane, 65
Sim, Rev., David, Presbyterian, 74
Simeon, Chronicler of Durham, 4
Simeon, Rev., Charles, 24
Simeon Trustees, 35, 37, 38, 44
Simes, Francis, 97, post office box-Holder 155
Simes, Mrs., 124
Simpson, John, 41
Simpson, Joshua, bell-ringer, 41
Sindi, owner of Bolling mentioned in Domesday Book, 219
Sion Baptist Church, The old Chapel, Goodman's End 66, illustration of 66, 67, 68, 124
"sitting up", custom of, 71
Skelton, Colonel, 207
Skelton, Thomas, Bradford Library, 97
Skerret, Mr., actor, 130-131, 171
Skerret, Mrs., actor, 130-131
Skerrit, actor, 171
Skerrit's Theatre, 130
Skinner Lane, 20, 40, 49, 122
Skipton, North Yorkshire, 10, 219
Skipton Castle, 219

Slack, Rev., Samuel, 81, 82
Slavery, 67, 88, 106, 188, Thomas Fowell Buxton, abolitionist 195, see William Wilberforce
Slave trade question, 67, 88, 180, 188, William Maud 213
Sleaford, Lincolnshire, 128
Sloane, Edward, humourist, 239
Sloane, Sir Hans, friend of Dr. Richardson, 222
Smallwood, Thomas, vicar of Idle, 47
Smedley, Mr., 128-129
"Smedley's" theatre, 128
Smith & Sons, dyers, 155
Smith-house, Lightcliffe, near Halifax, 73
Smith, John, bookseller, uncle of John Stanfield, 59, 69, 94, 156, 234
Smith, Mr., of Wainsgate, Baptist preacher, 62
Smith, Mr., actor, 134
Smith, Mr., pork butcher, 226
Smith, Ramsden W. rector of Hullcot, Bucks., 42
Smith, Rev., George Vance, of York, 51
Smith, Rev., John, 50, 69
Smith, Robert, innkeeper, Salutation Inn, 165
Smith, Samuel, "Blind Sam", 250
Smith, Samuel, Mayor, 86, 163, 190
Smithson, Mr., tobacconist, 225
Smithson, William, 103
Smith, T., 86
Smith W. & E., Post office box-holder, 155
Smith, Wilson & Co., 155
Smyth family, 205
Smyth, Thomas, 11
Smythson, Montague, actor, 143, 144
Snow, Francis, Landlord Rawson's Arms and the Nag's Head, 165, 174, 175
Socialists, (Socialism), 151, 247

Society of Friends, see Quakerism
Socinianism, 97, see Unitarianism
Soke, Right of local jurisdiction 6
Soke Mills, 123, 205, 213, 231, picture of the doorway of old Soke Mill 232
Soldier & Sailor Inn, also known as The Salutation Inn, 174
Southampton, 137
Southcott, Joanna, 58, 246
Southcottianism, 45, 245, 246, tracts and poems written against 246
Southey, Robert, 57
Southgate, later known as Sackville Street, 127
Southgate Hall, Westgate, 107
South Norwood, 242
Southowram, village in Calderdale, West Yorkshire, near Halifax, 93, 130
Sowden, John, artist, Preface xii
Sowden, Mr., actor, 134
Sowerby Bridge, Calderdale, West Yorkshire, 209
Speight, James, schoolteacher, 104
Spencer, Mr., printer, 234
Spinning-Jenny, 19
"Spotted House", Manningham Lane, 111, 250
Springthorpe's Waxwork and Magic Lantern Exhibitions, 151
Spurgeon, Rev., Charles Haddon, Baptist, 68
Staffordshire, county of, 179
Stage-coaches, see Coaches
Stamp, Rev., W. W., author of Wesleyan Methodism in Bradford and its Vicinity (1841), 61, 169
Stanfield, Charles, bookseller & printer, son of John Stanfield, 152, 226, 234
Stanfield, Clarkson, artist, 242
Stanfield, John, printer & stationer, 152, 226, 234
Stanfield Sons & Co., printers, 236
Stanhope, John, of Eccleshill,

"gentleman bearing arms" (1665), 201
Stanley, Dean, Anglican priest and Church historian, 87
Stanley, H, M, African explorer, 87
Stansfield, Elizabeth, daughter of Rev. Thomas Sharp of Horton Hall, 49
Stansfield, George, 121
Stansfield, Robert, dry-salter in Bradford, 49
Star Music Hall, Manchester Road, 43
Station Hotel, 225
Staunton, (Scruton probably means Stainton, Cumbria), 98
Staveley, Derbyshire, 221
Stead, John, 113
Steadman, Rev., William, minister of Westgate Baptist Church, 65, 66, 71, 84, 101, 102, 124, 213, mention of portrait by Geller 241
Steam-power, 21, 114
Steps Inn, 167
Sterne, Laurence, novelist and Anglican cleric, 95
Sthelwora, Johannes de, Medieval Poll Tax list, 12
Sticker Lane, Early school in 106
Stillingfleet, Rev., James, of Bierley Chapel, 69
Stirling, A, W, politician, 199
Stockwell orphanage, 68
Stoner, Rev., David, Methodist minister, 61
Stoney, Rev., R, of Dalton, Swedenborgian, 75
Storey, George, Landlord of King's Head Inn, 165
Storey, Robert, Craven-Dale poet, 171, 239
Stott Hill, 45, school at 106, old hall at 157, 203
Stott Hill House, 94, picture of between pages 202-203, description of 203
Stott Hill School, 106

Stott, Susannah, Mrs., Claiming use of armorial bearings (1798) 201
Stourport, North Worcestershire, 96
Stow, authority on the Medieval age, 9
Stoyle, J, D, actor, 136, 143, 144, picture of 144
Strafford, Thomas Wentworth, Earl of, 221
Strateburell, Richard, presbyter, 38
Strauss, Rev., Joseph, Rabbi, 76
Straw, Jack, Peasant's Revolt, 11
Strict Baptists, 68
Strikes & riots, Preface xii, 34, 54, 55, weavers and wool-combers strike (1825) 123, 159, 236
Stuff trade, 115
Sturdy, John, headmaster Bradford Grammar School, 79
Sturges, family, 218
Sturges, John, 222
Sturges & Co., 156
Subscription Library, see Bradford Subscription Library
Suffolk, county of, 37
Suffrage, extension of, 191
Sugden, John, Landlord of the Three Horse Shoes Inn, 174
Sullivan, Barry, actor, 149
Sunbridge, 37, 111, Sun Inn, 165, Roebuck Inn 165, Maud & Wilson Chemists 213, 229
Sunbridge Road, 231, 234
Sunday Schools, Horton Lane 70, 71, Moravian 74, 102-105, Kirkgate Wesleyan Sunday School, 103, parish Church Sunday School 103, Wesleyan Methodists 104, Baptists 104-104, Rev Crosse's Sunday School 118, involvement of William Maud 213
Sunderland, Mrs., illustrator, 88
Sunderland, Peter, "Gentleman bearing arms" (1665), 201
Sun Hotel, Ivegate, 122, 168, illustration of 170, 181, 182, headquarters of the Tories 188

Sun Inn, Sunbridge, 153, 165, 182
Surrey, County of, 205, 209
Sutcliffe, aged weaver, 244
Sutcliffe, Mr., 101
Sutcliffe, Rev., John, of Olney, 102
Swaine, Mr., J, 97
Swain Street, 89
Swales, Robert, 49
Swan Arcade, 172
Swanne, Ye, Public House, 164
Swedenborg, Emmanuel, Baron, 58, 75, his *True Christian Religion* 75
Swedenborgianism, (the New Church), 58, 75
Swift, Jonathan, 95
Swinbourne, Mr., actor, 147
Swinton Park, ancestral home of the Cunliffe-Lister family, Masham, near Harrogate, North Yorkshire, 180
Switzerland, 214
Syke, Robert de, Medieval Poll Tax list 11
Sykes, Colonel, William, MP, 82
Sykes, Daniel, 38
Sykes, Elizabeth, early Quaker, 52
Sykes, Jane, 38
Sykes, Joseph, 38
Sykes, Mabel, early Quaker, 52
Sykes, Rev., John, 38
Synagogue, 76

Tadcaster, North Yorkshire, 152, 175
Talbot Hotel, Kirkgate, 121, 124, 166, 170-171, illustration of 171, 177, 181, Headquarters of the Tories 188, 189
Tasker, Jonas, "eccentric verger", 166, 248
Taylor, Alice, daughter of Rev Christopher Taylor, 27
Taylor, John, 89, 92, 199
Taylor, Joshua, landlord of Duke of Wellington Inn, 165
Taylor, Laurence, Church clerk, 38
Taylor, Prof, 92
Taylor, Rev., Christopher, 27, 38
Taylor, Rev., J, 45-6, pamphlet war with Rev Francis Murphy, priest at St Mary's, Stott Hill
Taylor, Rev., Thomas, minister of Horton Lane Congregational Church, 70, 71, 72, 213, 239, mention of portrait by W. O. Geller 241
Taylor, the cooper, 228
Taylor, Thomas Rawson, son of Rev Thomas Taylor, poet, 71, 82, 100, 239
Technical College, 90, 107, 162, 216
Temperance Hall, 74, 150, 163, 213
Temperance Movement, 107, Bradford Long-pledged Teetotal Association 107, 247, total abstinence views of James Ellis and John Priestman 213, Reuben Holder 247
Tempest, Anne, daughter of Sir Richard, 221
Tempest, Beatrice, daughter of Sir Richard, wife of William Gascoigne of Shipley, 221
Tempest, Christopher, son of Sir Richard, 221
Tempest, Col., 111
Tempest, Elizabeth, daughter of Sir Richard, 221
Tempest, family of Bracewell near Skipton, 219
Tempest, family, Preface xii, 219, 220
Tempest, George, son of Sir Richard, 221
Tempest, Henry, son of Sir Richard, 221, 222
Tempest, Jane, daughter of Sir Richard, 221
Tempest, Mrs., Arthur, Preface xii
Tempest, Nicholas, 221
Tempest, Rosamond, daughter of

Tristram, 219, 221, see Rosamond de Bolling
Tempest, Sir, John, 205, 221
Tempest, Sir Richard, 24, 219, 220, 221
Tempest, Sir, Robert, son of Sir Richard, 221
Tempest, Sir, Thomas, son of Sir Richard, 221
Tempest, Tristram, son of Sir Richard, 221
Temple, Sir, William, historian, (*Introduction to English History*), 7
Ten Church Movement, 44
Ten Hours Bill, 42, 180, 218
Ten Hours Movement (Factory reform), 42, 218, John Wood's involvement in 218, Richard Oastler 218
Tetley, (Mr.,), 155
Tetley Street, Baptist Chapel in 68, 231
Tetley Street Baptist Church, 68
Tetley, William, 213
Thackeray, W. M., novelist and poet, 87
Thackley, northern suburb of Bradford, 52
Thalberg, musician, 163
Theatre Royal, Duke Street, 129, picture of 135, 130, 135, 136, 137, 141, 142, 143, 144, 145, 147, closure in 1867 147, 148, 174
Theatres, 125-149
"**The Bradford Instructive & Entertaining Miscellany**", 234
"**The New Borough Waits**", 250
Thirty Years War, 214
Thistlethwaite & Co., 156
Thompson, Benjamin, 160, 231
Thompson, Col. Thomas Peronnet, politician, later General, 187-188, 190, 191, 194, 198, picture of 199
Thompson, Gilbert, Fothergill's biographer, 211
Thompson, James, Post office box-Holder 155

Thompson, J. H., portrait painter, 243
Thompson, John, solicitor, 161, 207
Thompson, L. S., Proprietor of Market Building & Theatre, 119, 127, 128
Thompson, Lysander, actor, 127, 129, 136, 137, 139, 140, 144
Thompson, Matthew, father of M. W. Thompson, Mayor, 231, 250
Thompson, Matthew William, Mayor, 26, 90, 196-197, parliamentary election (1867) and (1869) 198, 208, laid foundation stone of the Town Hall 230, 231, 250
"**Thompson's Mill**", 231
Thompson's Theatre, 121, 127
Thoresby, 79, friend of Dr., Richardson 222
Thorne, Alicia, Medieval Poll Tax list 12
Thorne, Mr., & Mrs., strolling actors, 132
Thorne, Willelmus son of, Medieval Poll Tax list 11
Thorne's Theatre, 131, 133
Thornhill Green, near Huddersfield, 222
Thornton, family of, 8
Thornton, Henry, of Clapham, 24
Thornton, John, alias "Black Toppin", 111,
Thornton, John, Post office box-Holder 155, 165
Thornton Lane, 48
Thornton, Richard, early Quaker, 52, 113, 121
Thornton Road, 129, 150, old brewery 230, 231
Thornton Valley, 216
Thornton, West Bradford, 12, 47, Quakers at 52, Kipping Chapel at 69, 113, residence of Patrick Brontë 234
Thornton, William, 28
Thorp Arch, village near Bradford, 207, 208
Thorpe, George, draper, 227

Three Horse Shoes Inn, Tyrrel Street, 173, Illustration of 173
Tillotson, John, Archbishop of Canterbury, 209
Times, The, newspaper, 242
Tithes, 24-25
Tiverton, Devon, 190
Toad Lane, (Chapel Lane), 48, 152
Todmorden, Calderdale, West Yorkshire, 32, 34
Toll-Booth, Ivegate, 109, 110, 111, 226
Toller Lane, 76
Tolson & Tetley, post office box-holder, 155
Tolson, R., Post office box-holder 155
Tong, Bradford, 111, 124, 221, 222, Robert Carrick Wildon "the tailor poet of ...." 239
Tong Church, (Anglican), 124
Tong Hall, 111
Toole, J, L, actor, 149
Tooting, London, 24
Topham, F, W, artist, cousin to H. W. Topham, 243
Topham, F, W, W, son of F. W. Topham, artist, 243
Topham, Henry William, engraver, 242
Topham, Samuel, engraver, uncle of H. W. Topham, 242, 243
"Top o't taan Chapel", (Baptist), 21
Tordoff, Mr., tea dealer, 225
Tories (Toryism), 171, 179, 180, 181, 184, 185, 186, 187, 188
Torquay, Devon, 36
Total abstinence, see Temperance Movement
Tottenham, Quaker School at, 195
Tournay, 220
Tower of London, 31
Town Council, 160
Town-crier, 112
Town End, area of Bradford extending from Chapel Lane to the bottom of Horton Road, 20, 205
Town Hall, Preface xi, 162, 201, 230
Town Hill, 201
Town Hill House, also known as Duffield Hall, 218
Town Mission, 72
Town, Rev., Robert, of Haworth, 47
Towton, battle of (1461), 219
Tramways, 20
Tranter, organiser of a circulating library, 227
Trinity Chapel (Baptist), Horton Lane, 68
Trinity Church, Leeds, 24
Trinity College, Dublin, 36
Trout, Thomas, Post Master, 152
Trout, "Tommy", nephew of Thomas, 152
"tummies", pieces of cloth, 114
Turles, the, see Tyrrel Street
Turls Green, 59
Turner & Mitchell, firm of, 155
Turner, C. F., 155
Turner, Rev., Henry, 51
Turner, J. M. W., famous artist, 242
Turnpike Act, 176
Turnpike riots, 176, "Rebecca" rioters 176-177
Turnpike roads, 176-177
Tyburn, London, 221
Tyersal Moor-end, 176
Tyler, Wat, Peasant's Revolt, 11
Tyrrel Street, 8, 20, Sunday School in 103, 119, 161, Three Horse Shoes Inn165, New Inn 165, 173, 229, 230, prophet Wroe 244

Undercliffe, Bradford, 54, 56, 100, 214
Undercliffe House, 54, 106, 212
Unicorn Inn, Ivegate, 166, 217, 227
Uniformity Act, see Act of Uniformity (1662)
Union Passage, also known as Post Office Yard, Preface xi, 154,

illustration of 154, 156
Union Street, 104
Union, The, stage-coach, 177
Unitarian Chapel, Chapel Lane, 205
Unitarianism, 21, illustration of the gateway of old Unitarian Chapel 22, illustration of old Unitarian Chapel, in between 47-48, 69, 94, Socinianism 97, Unitarian Chapel 205
United Brethren, see Moravians
Universities 182-183, "Whig Universities" 186
University of Cambridge, 35, 207, 209, Clare College 209, Trinity College 209
University of Dublin, 186
University of Edinburgh, 72, 97, 211
University of Glasgow, 72
University of London, 75
University of Oxford, 190
Upwood, near Keighley, 184, 203

Vandenhoff, and his daughter, actors, 136, 138, 146, 147
Venice, Italy, 162
Verity, Dorothy, early Quaker, of Wibsey, 52
Vernon Gallery, Art, 242
Vicarage, Bradford parish, 27, illustration of the old vicarage 27
Vicar Lane, 28, 62
Vicars of Bradford, 28-38, catalogue of 38
Victoria, Queen, 82, read to by Amy Sedgwick 146, accession to the throne 183, confers baronet on Titus Salt 194
Vint, Rev., W. 99, 100-101
Virr, James, 49
Virtue, Mr., publisher, 242, "Gems of European Art" 242
Volunteer Corps, (formed 1794), 19
Vttyngwyf, Amica, Medieval Poll Tax List 12

Waddington, James, ("Ralph Goodwin") of Saltaire, poet, 239
Waddington, village in Lancashire, 220
Wade & Sons, James, 155
Wade, C. D., 171
Wade, James, innkeeper, the New Inn, 165, 170
Wade, James, treasurer of the Church Institution, 89
Wade, Joseph, 171
Wade, Mr., Sun Inn, 170
Wagstaff, J. Reid, solicitor, 85, 113, 155
Wagstaff, William, Landlord of Brown Inn, 165
Wainsgate, near Hebden Bridge, 62, Baptist Church at 63, 64
Wainwright, Mr., 88
"Waits", 250, Samuel Smith ("Blind Sam") 250, "The New Borough Waits" 250
Wakefield Bank, 159
Wakefield Cricket Club, 172
Wakefield Road, 54, 55, Duffield Hall 218
Wakefield, West Yorkshire, 12, 37, 47, 69, 73, 111, 126, 159, 210, 220, 137, 171, cricket club 172, Heath Hall 179, 205, 210, 220, Walton Hall 221, 233, mansion erected for prophet Wroe 246
Waldeck, German Principality, 214
Waldegrave, Thomas, of Bury St Edmunds, 99
Wales, Elkanah, curate of Pudsey, 47
Walker, Johannes, 12
Walker, Joshua, physician, 82
Walker, Miss, assistant librarian, 96
Walker, Rev., Samuel, 99
Walker, Ricardus, 11
Wallace, Rev., Dr., Alexander, Presbyterian, 74

Wallett, the "Queen's jester", strolling actor, 132, 133
Walmsley, boot maker, 227
Walmsley, Isaac, first Landlord of the Bermondsey Hotel, 174
"Walnut House", see Bolton Banks Farm
Walsh, Ed., 49
Walteri, Alicia, Medieval Poll Tax list 12
Walteri, Margaretta, Medieval Poll Tax List 12
"Walters Essart", 12 acres of land in Medieval Bolling, 219
Walton Hall, near Wakefield, 37, 171, 217, 221
Walton, Miss, actor, 130
Ward, Betty, school teacher, 50, 80
Ward, John, 113
Ward, Joseph, Landlord of Bowling Green Inn, 165, 167
Ward, Messrs, drapers, 189
Ward, Miss, of Bradford, Baptist benefactor, 102
Ward, Mr., student under John Fawcett, 101
Ward, Robert, 113
Ward, S. artist, Preface xii
Warde, Miles, 29
Wardlaw, Dr., His *"Systematic Theology"* 72
Wardman, Benjamin, Landlord of the Boy & Barrel Inn, 165
Wardman, Henry, Wesleyan, printer, 234
Warham, Norfolk, 207
Warrior, C., chemist, Kirkgate, See picture between 224-225
Wars of the Roses, 1, 13, 218, 219
Watchmen, 21
Waterhouse, Anna, wife of Rev. Jonas Waterhouse, 203
Waterhouse, "Bob", in Bank Street, 185
Waterhouse, George, 205
Waterhouse, Mr., Landlord of the "Bull's Head" Inn, then later Armstrong's Hotel in Horton Lane, 243
Waterhouse, Rev., Jonas, vicar of Bradford, 31, 38, ejectment (1662) 47, 203
"Waters Essart", land in Bolling, 219
Waterton, Sir Thomas, married Jane Tempest, 221
Watson, Joseph, teacher at Bradford Grammar School and later the post master, 156
Watson, Mr., M., 83
Watson, Messrs, shopkeepers, 225
Waud & Co., C., 155
Waud, G, Motley, politician, 199
Waugh, Edwin, 161, 238
Weardley, near Harewood, West Yorkshire, birthplace of the poet John Nicholson, 237, picture of the cottage in which Nicholson was born 238
Weavers and Woolcomber's strike, (1825), see Strikes and riots
Webbester, John, presbyter, 38
Webster, Adam, Medieval Poll Tax list 12
Webster, Johanna, Medieval Poll Tax list, 11
Weddall, John, 27
Wells, William, post office box-holder, 155
Well Street, 79, 85, 128, Ship Inn, 165, 174
Wennington Hall, Lancashire, 110
Wensleydale, North Yorkshire, 211
Wentworth & Co., Bank, 160, illustration of Wentworth & Co., Market Street 160, 161
Wentworth, Rishworth & Chaloners, (Wentworth Bank), 159
Wentworth, Thomas, Earl of Strafford, 221
Wesleyan Academy, near Bradford, 40
Wesleyan Methodism, Octagon

Chapel 21, 57-62, Sunday Schools 104, hiring by the Oddfellows lodge 151, Henry Wardman 234

Wesleyan Reformers, 62, 151

Wesley, Rev., John, founder of Methodism, 32, 47, 57, 58, 59, 60, 64, 69, picture of Wesley preaching 76, 94, 97, 168, his view on Turnpike roads 176, 249

Westgate, 3, 8, 20, 40, 46, 53, 64, 65, William Steadman and Benjamin Godwin, 66, 67, 68, 69, Southgate Hall, 107, old justice court 110, 111, 118, 119, 120, 124, 127, market held at bottom of 152, 152, Pack Horse Inn 165, The Angel Inn 165, Bull's Head Inn 165, Hare & Hounds Inn, 165, King's Head Inn,165, Old Bishop Blaize Inn, 165, Saracen's Head Inn, 165, Bull's Head Inn 168, residence of Robert Milligan 189, 195, 200, 201, 208, Bartlett family 210-211, William Maud, chemist, practiced in 213, shops in Westgate 225, picture of shops 226, 233, John Stanfield's printing shop 234, picture of old shops between 234-235, 236, bookshop of Abraham Holroyd 238, old Judy Barrett's spice shop 248

Westgate Baptist Church, Known as "top-o-taan Chapel" 21, William Crabtree 63, 64, led by William Steadman, 65, John Rushton sings at 247

Westminster Review, 188

Weston, William, (1541), 38

West Riding Advertiser, 235

West Riding Session Rolls, Wakefield, 210

Wharfe-dale, 15

Wharfe Tavern, Bolton Road, 81

Wharton & Co., 155

Wharton, Joshua, Post office box-Holder 155

Wheat Sheaf Inn, Wakefield Road, 218

Wheeler, Esther, wife of Benjamin Seebohm, 214

Wheeler, Fidelity, 214

Wheeler, Joshua, fellow prisoner with John Bunyan in Bedford gaol, 214

Wheeler, Joshua, of Hitchen, 214

Wheeler, Mary, wife of James Ellis, 214

Wheeler, Sarah, 214

Whetley Hill, Bradford, 3, 20, 30

Whigs, (political party), 179, 180, 181, 184, 185, 186

Whitaker & Co., William, 155, 231

Whitaker, Dr., local historian, 2, 6, 9, reference to his "Loidis and Elmete" 201

Whitaker, Elizabeth, daughter of William Whitaker, married Benjamin Thompson, 231

Whitaker, John, first librarian in Bradford, 95

Whitaker, Richard, distinguished himself as a soldier at Corunna, 231

Whitaker, William, father of Elizabeth, 231

Whitby, North Yorkshire, 34

White Abbey, district of Bradford, 8, 44, Sunday School in 103, 136

Whitefield, (Whitfield), Rev., George, revival preacher, Calvinist, 58, 59, visits Bradford, 64, 69, 97, 168

White Horse Inn, Kirkgate, 166, 175

White House, at the foot of the Church steps, Bradford, 80, 96

White Lion, dram shop, 175

White Lion Inn, Kirkgate, 114, 162, 166, 175, 184

White Swan Inn, Halifax, 153

White Swan Inn, Market Street, 166, 172, illustration of 173, 177, 227

Whitlam, Caroline, wife of Sir Titus

Salt, 215
Whitlam, George, of Great Grimsby, Caroline's father, 215
Whitworth, Mr., Sun Hotel, 170
Wiber, Miss, actress, 148
Wibsey, district of Bradford, 48, 52, 56, 74, 111, 172
Wibsey Bank Foot, 176
Wickham, Col., of Cottingley, 189
Wickham, Henry W., (AKA Henry Hird), son of Rev., Lamplugh Hird, 187, 189-191, 193, 195, 196, 198, 207
Wickham, L. W., son of Rev., Lamplugh Hird, 207
Wilberforce, William, son of the famous philanthropist, 186, 187, 188, 198
Wild boar, see Boar Legend
Wild, "Jemmy", itinerant theatrical entertainer, 128, 132
Wild, Mrs., 135
Wilde, Mr., co-lessee of the Royal Alexandra Theatre, 149
Wildman, Abraham, poet, 239
Wildon, Robert Carrick, the "tailor-poet of Tong", 239
Wilkes, John, 179
Wilkinson, Benjamin, 113
Wilkinson, John, "Gentleman bearing arms" (1665), 201
Willelmi, Alicia, Medieval Poll Tax list 12
Willelmi, Robertus, Medieval Poll Tax list 12
Willelmi, Thomas, Medieval Poll Tax List 12
Willet, Oxley & Co., 155
Willet, Thomas, Post office box-holder 155
Willey, Mr., 136
William and Mary, Monarchs, 19
William IV, King, 181, 183, 241
William, the Conqueror, 4
Willis, Rev., Dr., H., de L., 43
Willit & Co., Thomas, 155
"Will Lee Hoil", the debtors 112
Wills, at York, 28
Wills, early Bradford, Preface xii, 28, 29
Wilman, Mr., Landlord, The Sun Inn, 170
Wilsden, Richard de, presbyter, 38
Wilson, Anderson, J, local artist, 129, 130, 240, 243
Wilson, Elizabeth, Landlady, Shoulder of Mutton Inn, 165
Wilson, Mr., silversmith, 225
Wilson, Quaker family, 54
Wilson, Richard Fountayne, MP, 124
Wilson, Robert, 48
Wilson, William, "Quaker Wilson", 212-213
Wilton, John, clothes-broker, 226
Windermere, Cumbria, 37
Winn, see Wynn, early Quaker
Wolsey, (June 1513), 220
Wood & Walker, Messrs, firm of, 42, 207, 218
Wood, Arthur, actor, 148
Wood, family, 218
Wood, Francis Lindley, 222
Wood, George, 89
Wood, James, provider of bell-rope, 41
Wood, John, manufacturer and philanthropist, Snr and Jnr., 42, 121, 160, 217, factory reform 218
Wood, John, schoolmaster, 235
Wood, Mr., 42
Wood, Rebecca, Landlady Talbot Hotel, 166
Wood, Rev., Benjamin, Baptist, 68
Wood, Thomas, 94
Wood, William, 160
Wood & Walker, firm, 42, 155
Woodhouse Grove School, 40
Woolgar, Mr., & Miss, actors, 137
Woolmer, John, owner of Bowling Green Inn, 167
Woolpacks' Inn, Preface xi, picture of in-between 164-165, 174

Wool trade, 19, 115-116, 208, 214, 215
Workhouse, 112-14, illustration of old workhouse Barkerend, 113
Worsted trade, 19, 115, 180, origins in Norfolk 206, power-loom 206, 208 spinning-frame 206, 213, 231
"Wren, Jenny", poet, 239
Wright, Dr., 94
Wright, Isaac, Post office box-holder 155
Wright, John, Landlord of Dog & Shovel Inn, 165
Wright, John, father of Thomas Wright of Birkenshaw, 167
Wright, Matthew, early Quaker, a clothier of Bradford, 52, 53
Wright, Thomas, grandfather of Thomas Wright of Birkenshaw, 167
Wright, Thomas, of Birkenshaw, 50, 80, 161, his autobiography 167
Wroe, John, prophet, 58, 244-246, picture of 245, mansion erected for 246
Wycliffe Society, 210
Wykeham, William of, bishop of Winchester, 189
Wynceby, William de, 38
Wynn, John, Quaker, Persecuted 19, 53
Wyrill, Mr., ironmonger, 85, 225
Wyrill, Thomas, early member of Horton Lane Congregational Church, 70

Yewdall, Zachariah, early Quaker, 52
Yewdalls, Quaker family of Eccleshill and Idle, 54
York, 2, 13, 28, 29, 35, 45, 51, 57, 78, 92, 102, 140, 142, 175, 189, 217, 219, 221, 222, 233, 235
York Archiepiscopal Registers, 37
York Castle, 186
Yorkshire Archaeological Journal, footnote 11
Yorkshire Banking Co., 161
Yorkshire District Bank, 155
Yorkshire Penny Bank, 162
Young, Mr., Arthur, his "*Tours*", 176

Zoar Baptist Church, Westgate, 68, 249
Zuccareth, artist, 242

References

[1] Promotional pre-publication leaflet, in Scruton's Scrapbook, West Yorkshire Archive Service (WYAS), Bradford, ref. DB5/C31.

[2] Our main sources for Scruton's life include J. C. Handby, *Bradford Antiquary*, October, 1927, vol., 7, William Scruton, obituary; Pen Portrait 31, *Yorkshire Notes & Queries*, No 7, vol. III, October 1906; Census Reports, Wade Hustwick, and snippets of information gained in his Scrapbooks, ref. DB5/C31; 34WYB314 and WYB364 (WYAS).

[3] Handby, *Bradford Antiquary,* October, 1927, op.cit., p. 73.

[4] Pen Portrait 31, *Yorkshire Notes & Queries*, October 1906, op.cit

[5] J. C. Handby, "William Scruton 1840-1924", *Bradford Antiquary*, op.cit., p. 73.

[6] Pen Portrait 31, *Yorkshire Notes & Queries*, op.cit.

[7] J. C. Handby, "William Scruton 1840-1924", *Bradford Antiquary*, op.cit., p. 74.

[8] Jack Reynolds, Introduction, W. Scruton, *Pen & Pencil Pictures of Old Bradford*, The Amethyst Press, Otley, 1985.

[9] Scruton was buried in Scholemoor Cemetery and Crematorium, plot Sec 5, No. 496 Uncon, Memorial ID 126311618

[10] *Thornton and the Brontës*, 1898. Printed by Sewell, see Pen Portrait 31, *Yorkshire Notes & Queries,* No 7, vol. III, October 1906, op.cit.

[11] W. Scruton, *Pen and Pencil Pictures of Old Bradford,* T. Brear, Bradford, 1889, p. xii.

[12] J. Reynolds & W.F. Baines, "One Hundred Years Of Local History", *Bradford Antiquary*,1978, p. 26.

[13] Scruton, *Pen and Pencil Pictures of Old Bradford,* 1889, op.cit., Preface, p. xi.

[14] *Pen and Pencil Pictures*, ibid., Preface, ibid., p. xi.

[15] Ibid., p. 216.

[16] Ibid., p. 230.

[17] Ibid., Preface, p. xi.

[18] Ibid., Preface, p. xi.

[19] "Prospectus", promotional flysheet, 1889, Scrapbook, WYA, class No 33, Deed Box 5.

[20] Prospectus, promotional flysheet, 1889, op.cit.

[21] Scruton, *Pen and Pencil Pictures of Old Bradford,* 1889, op.cit., p. 19.

[22] *Pen and Pencil Pictures of Old Bradford,* Ibid., p. 31.

[23] Ibid., p. 48.

[24] Ibid., p. 103.

[25] Ibid., p. 131.

[26] Ibid., p. 143.

[27] Ibid., p. 129.

[28] Ibid., pp. 168, 171, 172,177.

[29] Ibid., p. 4.

[30] Ibid., p. 28.

[31] Ibid., p. 164
[32] Ibid., pp. 24, 37.
[33] Ibid., p. 3.
[34] Ibid., pp. 13, 201.
[35] Ibid., p. 15.
[36] Ibid., pp. 48, 80.
[37] Ibid., p. 157.
[38] Ibid., p. 115.
[39] Ibid., p. 214.
[40] The majority of Scruton's scrapbooks can be found under DB5/C31 - 34, as well as WYB314 and WYB364 in the WYAS, Bradford.
[41] For Titus Salt see the large dark brown, untitled volume, scrapbook ref 38D96/1, Scrapbooks DB5, WYAS, Bradford
[42] See for example the scrapbook titled William Scruton of Bradford, Scrapbook of autographed photographs, engravings and documents relating to prominent Victorians and local people, WYAS, Bradford, ref 38D96

Printed in Great Britain
by Amazon